Key Concepts in
Sport & Exercise
Sciences

The SAGE Key Concepts series provides students with accessible and authoritative knowledge of the essential topics in a variety of disciplines. Cross-referenced throughout, the format encourages critical evaluation through understanding. Written by experienced and respected academics, the books are indispensable study aids and guides to comprehension.

DAVID KIRK, CARLTON COOKE,
ANNE FLINTOFF AND JIM MCKENNA

Key Concepts in
Sport & Exercise
Sciences

Los Angeles • London • New Delhi • Singapore

First published 2008

SAGE Publications Ltd
1 Oliver's Yard
55 City Road
London EC1Y 1SP

SAGE Publications Inc.
2455 Teller Road
Thousand Oaks, California 91320

SAGE Publications India Pvt Ltd
B 1/I 1 Mohan Cooperative Industrial Area
Mathura Road, New Delhi 110 044

SAGE Publications Asia-Pacific Pte Ltd
33 Pekin Street #02-01
Far East Square
Singapore 048763

Library of Congress Control Number: 2008922645

British Library Cataloguing in Publication data

A catalogue record for this book is available from the British Library

ISBN 978-1-4129-2227-2
ISBN 978-1-4129-2228-9 (pbk)

Typeset by C&M Digitals (P) Ltd., Chennai, India
Printed in India at Replika Press Pvt. Ltd.
Printed on paper from sustainable resources

The editors dedicate this book to all of the students and staff they have worked with and learned from over many years of teaching sport and exercise sciences.

contents

contents

key concepts in
sport & exercise sciences

list of contributors

We would like to thank all of the people who have contributed to this book upon the request of the editors; their help and support is greatly appreciated.

Susan Backhouse, Leeds Metropolitan University
Nassos Bissas, Leeds Metropolitan University
Peter Bramham, Leeds Metropolitan University
Ron Butterly, Leeds Metropolitan University
David Carless, Leeds Metropolitan University
Steve Cobley, Leeds Metropolitan University
Carlton Cooke, Leeds Metropolitan University
Chris J. Cushion, Loughborough University
Hayley Fitzgerald, Leeds Metropolitan University
Anne Flintoff, Leeds Metropolitan University
Mike Gray, Leeds Metropolitan University
Brian Hanley, Leeds Metropolitan University
Kevin Hylton, Leeds Metropolitan University
Theocharis Ispoglou, Leeds Metropolitan University
Rod King, Leeds Metropolitan University
David Kirk, Leeds Metropolitan University
Jonathan Long, Leeds Metropolitan University
Christopher Low, Leeds Metropolitan University
Suzanne McGregor, Leeds Metropolitan University
Jim McKenna, Leeds Metropolitan University
Ann MacPhail, University of Limerick
Adam Nicholls, University of Hull
Terry O'Donnell, Leeds Metropolitan University
Toni O'Donovan, Leeds Metropolitan University
Mary O'Flaherty, Mayo Education Centre and University of Limerick
John O'Hara, Leeds Metropolitan University
Andy Pringle, Leeds Metropolitan University
Adrian Schonfeld, Leeds Metropolitan University
Karl Spracklen, Leeds Metropolitan University
Sarah Squires, Leeds Metropolitan University
Louise Sutton, Leeds Metropolitan University
Beccy Watson, Leeds Metropolitan University
Cathy Zanker, Leeds Metropolitan University

Introduction

Over the past 30 years the number of courses in sport, exercise and related topics has grown enormously, making sport currently one of the most popular fields of study in schools, colleges and universities. Many of these courses involve multidisciplinary study of sport and exercise, crossing the biophysical sciences, social and psychological sciences and the humanities. Part of the popularity of courses in sport and exercise is due to the variety that multidisciplinary study provides. But the sheer range and diversity of disciplines involved is also very challenging for students.

Alongside this growth in popularity of school and university courses, research activity has also increased, creating a mini 'knowledge explosion' in sport and exercise. Where once only a few general journals served the sport and exercise research community, now there are usually several journals in each of the specialist areas of study. For students beginning their course of study in sport and exercise, mastering this large and growing body of diverse specialist knowledge can be a bewildering and daunting prospect.

This book seeks to serve as a reader-friendly source of Key Concepts in five of the main areas of study in sport and exercise courses: biomechanics, exercise physiology, pedagogy, psychology and sociology. Each section of the book contains entries on the concepts that organise each of these areas of study. Understanding these concepts is the starting point for understanding sport and exercise more broadly and will allow students beginning their courses to move on to acquire more specialised knowledge. It will also serve as a useful means of preparing for examinations and other forms of assessment for those undertaking more advanced studies who need to refresh their memories.

Each of the entries is concise, explaining in easily accessible language the essential ideas of each of the areas of study in sport and exercise. Serving as a starting point for more advanced study, each entry also offers one or two references for further reading, where each Key Concept is explained in more depth.

So the book is intended primarily for students beginning their college and university courses in sport and exercise sciences, physical education and related topics such as leisure and sport development. It will also provide a valuable and challenging introduction to key ideas for students of A Level physical education and sports studies.

The editors and most of the entry writers are members of academic staff at Leeds Metropolitan University's Carnegie Faculty of Sport and Education. The faculty traces its origins to the Carnegie Physical Training College. Carnegie has been a byword for excellence in sport and physical education since it opened its doors in October 1933. In its 75th year (2008–9), Carnegie is the provider of the most comprehensive range of undergraduate and postgraduate courses in sport and related topics in Britain, including many foundation degrees offered by partner further education colleges in its unique Regional University Network. Supported by colleagues in other well-known institutions for the study of sport, the editors and writers bring all of their research expertise and experience of teaching on these courses to the preparation of this book.

PART I

Biomechanics

INTRODUCTION

Biomechanics is the area of sport and exercise science where the laws, principles and methods of mechanics are applied to the structure and function of the human body. Mechanics can be divided into two categories: statics, which is the study of stationary objects, and dynamics, which is the study of moving objects. Examples of static analysis in sport include standing, different balances in gymnastics and acrobatics and certain resistance exercises where no movement is apparent but large forces may be exerted such as in a scrum in rugby or a closely matched tug-of-war contest. Most activities in physical activity and sport involve movement and therefore require the application of dynamics to understand that movement.

Two other subdivisions are often used to describe different levels of biomechanical analysis: **Kinematics**, which is a description of the movement in terms of time and space, and kinetics, which is concerned with an explanation of the underlying mechanics of the movement and typically involves an assessment of forces. Kinematic analyses in sport typically rely on images recorded by video and other cameras, which can be played back many times either at normal speed or frame by frame, pausing on key frames that show important aspects of the technique. Kinetic analyses in sport and exercise also employ images, but supplement these with force plates and other force transducers, that allow the forces exerted against the ground or on sports equipment to be measured. An example of kinetic analysis related to health is gait analysis, which typically combines ground reaction force data captured as an individual steps on and off a force plate synchronised with frame-by-frame images recorded by a camera. Such an analysis may help a podiatrist to diagnose the cause of problems in walking, where the data collected can assist in prescribing orthotics, which are inserts to go into shoes to help alleviate problems in walking. A typical example from sport would also combine frame-by-frame images synchronised with force measurements, such as the video recording of a kayak paddling stroke, while simultaneously recording the magnitude and direction of the forces exerted on the shaft of the paddle.

The following entries introduce the different components of biomechanics and will help students gain a good understanding of how to analyse movement and learn how to explain how it is produced. The ability to separate good and bad elements of the mechanics of techniques and style is a requirement for all biomechanists who wish to be able to explain how movement patterns in physical activity and sport can be improved.

CARLTON COOKE

Kinematics

Video analysis has become a very popular method to assess sports performance. The recording and repeated observation of motion captured by video cameras is relatively straightforward, especially now that the technology is so readily available and feedback on what has been recorded is immediate via playback through the camera.

However, there are different approaches to motion analysis, which are characterised by the principles and methodology underpinning them. Qualitative analysis (non-numerical and descriptive) is based entirely on visual observation of a movement, sequence of movements or a game performance and it draws its validity from the knowledge and experience of the person who observes and analyses the selected motion. In contrast a quantitative approach (numerical analysis) guarantees objective results as long as the correct mechanical principles and scientific methodology are used. The branch of **Biomechanics** that describes human or object motion mainly via image analysis is called kinematics. Kinematics describes motion in terms of space and time, and it provides valuable information regarding the position and the rate of movement of the human body, its segments or any implement used in a sport and exercise situation.

TYPES OF MOTION AND MECHANICAL QUANTITIES

The pathway of the motion experienced by moving bodies can be described as either straight line (rectilinear motion), or curved line (curvilinear motion) or they can rotate about an axis (*angular motion*). For example, an ice hockey player gliding straight across the ice with the same posture will result in all the segments of his body moving the same distance over the same time period (translation). In addition a discus travelling in the air following a curved path is an example of *linear motion* since its motion is translational too. In contrast, a gymnast who rotates around the high bar with a straight body position undergoes rotation about an external fixed axis where all the body segments travel through the same angle, in the same direction, in the same time, but covering different curvilinear distances with the segments further away from the axis (e.g. feet) travelling further than the segments closer to the axis (e.g. shoulders). There are also occasions where angular motion is observed with respect to an imaginary axis, which in many events could be located outside the physical boundaries of the human body (e.g. rotations in gymnastics or diving about the centre of gravity during flight). However, the most common form of motion in sport and exercise is a combination of angular and linear motion; this is called *general motion*. For instance in cycling, some body segments (e.g. thighs and legs) and parts of the bicycle (wheels) undergo rotation about joints of the body and the centre of the wheel respectively, whereas other body segments (e.g. hips and head) and bicycle parts (e.g. bicycle frame) undergo translation with the total movement of the system (bicycle and cyclist) being linear.

Once the type of motion has been established the kinematic analysis can be performed by applying mechanical principles and formulae that provide information about the changes in the distance covered, the speed of movement and temporal pattern of the movement. In other words, by using vector quantities (magnitude and direction) instead of scalar (magnitude), the *position displacement, velocity* and *acceleration* of a body and/or object can be measured and expressed in S.I. units by using the same techniques and formulae for both angular and linear kinematics. The names, symbols and specific units differ between linear and angular quantities to allow inclusion of the characteristics of each type of motion. For example, the definition of velocity is the rate at which a body changes its position with respect to time and it can be obtained if the change in displacement is divided by the time taken for the change in displacement. In linear motion this velocity is denoted by the Latin letter v and it is measured in $m.s^{-1}$. In angular motion it is denoted by the Greek letter ω and it is measured in $rad.s^{-1}$ since the change in angular position is represented by the change in angle measured in radians (radians are used because they provide a means of calculating linear velocity of any point rotating around an axis by using the equation $v = \omega r$, where v is linear velocity ($m.s^{-1}$), ω is angular velocity ($rad.s^{-1}$) and r is the radius (m). There are 2π radians in 360°).

ANALYSING MOVEMENT IN PHYSICAL ACTIVITY AND SPORT

One of the main uses of biomechanics in sport and exercise science is in the analysis of patterns of human movement in either physical activity or sport. General movement patterns have common elements in terms of segment movements, axes of rotation and planes of movement and are easily recognised by most people and described as walking, running, jumping, throwing, catching, striking and kicking. When a general movement pattern is adapted for use in a particular physical activity or sport it is a skill. Taking the example of jumping, the high jump would be a particular skill within the general group of movement patterns we would all recognise as jumps. There are of course different ways of performing the high jump, with most children starting with a scissor jump and most, if not all, international high jumpers performing the Fosbury flop (named after its originator, high jumper Dick Fosbury). Different ways of performing a skill are called techniques, so that the scissor jump and Fosbury flop represent examples of very different high jump techniques. Each of these techniques would have common elements, which make them relatively easy for us to categorise as particular forms of high jump technique. However, if you watch international high jumpers performing the Fosbury flop, you will observe that not all jumpers execute the Fosbury flop in exactly the same way. Rather, they have adapted or modified the technique; and these individual differences and adaptations are known as the style of the performer. Skill, technique and style are developed as a function of the requirements and constraints of a particular event such as the high jump (e.g. the rules of high jumping that require a one-leg take-off; the shape of the high jump area, which allows for a curved approach; the size, shape and fitness of the jumper, which are human constraints; and the coach, who may develop the Fosbury flop with an emphasis on certain aspects of the technique).

APPLICATIONS OF KINEMATICS

There is a wide spectrum of applications of linear and angular kinematics in sport and exercise. These applications are extremely valuable in motion analysis, especially now that advanced technology has improved the equipment that is used to obtain kinematic data. The employment of high-speed video systems in conjunction with sophisticated software, which converts the captured images into two- and three-dimensional coordinates, enables the sports biomechanist to obtain accurate estimates of instantaneous values of the kinematic variables critical in the performance of a movement or sequence of movements. The calculation of instantaneous rather than average values of a given quantity (e.g. velocity) distinguishes quantitative kinematic analysis from qualitative observation. In most analyses of sport it is much more informative to determine the characteristics of a performance at a particular instant in time. For instance, the linear velocities of the centre of gravity and its projection angle with respect to the horizontal at the instant of take-off in long jump will determine to a large extent the distance jumped by the athlete. There are numerous examples of the use of kinematic analyses right across the range of sport and exercise performances. On many occasions the use of kinematic analysis is significant in examining sporting movements that rely extensively on the performance of correct and effective technique, such as in a tennis serve or a javelin throw. Data from a kinematic analysis of these two movements can provide the coach and the performer with valuable information on technique, but also inform recommendations with respect to corrections and adjustments that can lead to performance enhancement. Kinematic analysis has also proved successful in health-related applications, especially those that examine the effects of body posture and the specific movement patterns on the musculoskeletal system during different sport and recreational activities. The outcome of these applications is typically:

1 identification of the source of a problem affecting the performer (e.g. overpronation in running)
2 measures and advice on how to reduce or prevent the problem which, in running for example, might include a change of footwear or the prescription of an orthotic insert by a podiatrist.

When analysing movement a sound understanding of the laws, principles and methods of biomechanics can enable students to observe and explain which elements of technique and style are effective in optimising the movement and which need to be changed to produce a better movement pattern, either in terms of performance or prevention of injury. For example, a discus thrower who leans backwards as she makes the first turn at the back of the circle, will most probably translate that backward lean to the throwing position at the front of the circle. This will result in a loss of power and therefore velocity at the point of release. For a right-handed thrower leaning back through the delivery phase, the point of release will occur too soon and the discus will land towards the right line of the sector or, worse still, hit the cage or go out of the sector, producing a foul throw. An explanation of such errors in style and technique can only be made with good observational skills coupled with the application of biomechanics.

FURTHER READING

Hamill, J. and Knutzen, K.M. (2003) *Biomechanical Basis of Human Movement*, 2nd edn. Philadelphia, PA: Lippincott, Williams & Wilkins.

Watkins, J. (2007) *Introduction to Biomechanics of Sport and Exercise*. Oxford: Elsevier Health Sciences.

Zatsiorsky, V. (1998) *Kinematics of Human Motion*. Champaign, IL: Human Kinetics.

NASSOS BISSAS
CARLTON COOKE

Force

KINETICS

Understanding force is essential to understanding movement, not just in a sporting context but also in everyday activities. While kinematics is about describing movement and kinetics is about explaining cause and effect in movement, understanding force is a key component of kinetics. Force is a vector quantity and so it has magnitude and direction associated with it.

FORCE AND ACCELERATION

Put very simply, a force is something that causes acceleration. Acceleration in everyday terms is usually understood to mean speeding up, but in biomechanics it is more correct to say it means a change in velocity. Because velocity is a measure of how fast something is moving in a straight line, it is possible to change velocity (and hence to accelerate) by:

- speeding up;
- slowing down;
- changing direction.

It is common for a combination of these to occur, for example, a snooker ball hitting the cushion will tend to slow down and change direction.

Acceleration with an increase in velocity is usually known as positive acceleration, with a decrease it is called negative acceleration or deceleration.

If you consider different examples where people or implements speed up, slow down, or change direction, it is possible to identify quite easily what forces are acting in order to cause this acceleration. For example, a ball kicked along the grass will slow down due to friction; a strong wind (air resistance) can cause a rugby ball to deviate from its course; and a tennis ball thrown before serving will slow down as it goes upwards, stop, change direction, and speed back up again all due to gravity. Forces cannot be seen but their effects can, and it is useful to remember that whenever something accelerates there is an unseen force acting in order to make this happen.

The quantity of force that occurs during acceleration can be calculated by multiplying the mass of the object being affected by the acceleration it undergoes. This can be written as an equation:

$$\text{Force} = \text{mass (kg)} \times \text{acceleration (m.s}^{-2}\text{)}$$

This can also be written as:

$$\text{Force} = \text{mass} \times \text{change in velocity} / \text{time taken}$$

FORCES AND INJURY RISK

When two bodies collide, with one or both moving, an impact occurs and this force causes acceleration as described before. In sporting activities, this can cause injury or other damage if the forces are relatively large. The human body is relatively weak in preventing injury due to impact because of the nature of soft tissue such as muscle.

Taking the second equation above into consideration, we can consider ways in which to reduce these impact forces. Reducing velocity is generally the opposite of what is required for sporting success, so we will ignore that option. The alternative is to increase the time taken for the impact to occur. This is one of the concepts that is used in the design of a vast amount of sporting footwear. Cushioning in the soles of the shoes deforms during foot contact with the ground and this slow deformation reduces the impact forces.

A rugby player could also reduce the impact forces upon him when tackling another player by increasing the time over which the impact occurs. The problem with this is that by taking more time to complete the tackle, the opposition player will gain more distance forwards. In games like rugby and American football, losing distance like this to the opposition is typically detrimental. As a result, rugby players will tend to tackle hard (the impact occurring over a very short time) with the consequential risk of injury. American football has tried to overcome this problem of needing high impact forces to stop the opposition while preventing injury through the use of substantial body padding. The padding is designed to be hard on the outside (so that the impact forces on the opposition are high) while being cushioned on the inside (so that the impact forces on the player wearing it are low). Problems with this approach can occur when helmets for protection are used as ways of increasing impact in contact.

IMPULSE

Production of a high force does not always result in a large amount of acceleration. The amount of time spent applying that force is also of importance. The product of force and the time over which it acts is defined as impulse. For example, if the brakes are applied in a car for a very short time, there may be a slight jerk in the car's movement but it won't completely stop. What is needed is for the time duration of force application to be increased so that full deceleration is complete. The impulse of a force can also be said to be the change in momentum. With our example of the car, the higher the deceleration impulse, the greater the change in the car's momentum (in effect its speed because mass will change negligibly). Research on sprint starts has shown that bunch starts, with the feet placed closed together in the starting blocks, give the fastest clearance at the gun. However, placing the feet further apart results in a higher overall running speed to 10m because although the initial explosive force is less, the impulse is greater due to the legs having longer to push from the blocks.

PRESSURE

Quite often it is not the amount of force applied that causes damage or injury, but the amount of pressure. Pressure is the amount of force applied with regard to the area over which it is applied. A player wear-ing football boots will apply more pressure to the ground as compared to a player wearing normal trainers because of the small surface area of the studs. Increasing pressure in this way is beneficial in that it allows breaking of the grass surface and the resulting improvement in traction. However it can be detrimental in that the reaction force exerted onto the foot is not spread evenly but instead applied at perhaps six or eight separate points. This effect is not usually noticed on soft surfaces like turf but can be important on harder ground such as that experienced during dry weather.

FURTHER READING

Kreighbaum, E. and Barthels, K.M. (1996) *Biomechanics: A Qualitative Approach for Studying Human Movement*, 4th edn. Minneapolis: Burgess Publishing Company.
Watkins, J. (2007) *Introduction to Biomechanics of Sport and Exercise*. Oxford: Elsevier Health Sciences.
Zatsiorsky, V. (2002) *Kinetics of Human Motion*. Champaign, IL: Human Kinetics.

BRIAN HANLEY

Impacts

Impacts are common in the world of sport. Many impacts are desirable because, for instance, of the need to move the human body (e.g. impact between the feet and ground in running), to score points (e.g. impact between the board and the ball in basketball), or just to continue a game by passing the ball (e.g. impact between the foot and the ball in football). The list with examples that demonstrate the critical and essential role of impacts in sports can be extended to include almost every single sport played today. Most sports have been designed and developed by using impacts as the means by which the execution of the sport-specific movements are achieved. In many sports there are different types of impact taking place, which are affected by a variety of factors.

For example in tennis, the impact between the tennis racquet and the ball is influenced by factors such as the mass and elasticity of the two impacting bodies, the ball velocity, the angle of impact and the type of ball spin. The impact between the tennis player's feet and the ground is influenced by the elasticity of both bodies, the impact angle, the frictional characteristics of the tennis surface used (i.e. grass, clay or synthetic). In addition a third type of impact occurs in tennis when the ball contacts the ground and this is affected by all the factors mentioned above for the other two impacts.

MECHANICS OF IMPACT

Impacts between two bodies can be divided into direct and oblique impacts. Direct ones are those that occur when *a)* one moving body strikes one stationary body after it has travelled along a path that forms a right angle with the second body's surface (a volleyball lands on the ground) or *b)* the two bodies are in motion and they have travelled along the same straight line prior to the impact (a defender's header against an oncoming ball in football). Oblique impacts are those which occur when *a)* a moving body impacts a stationary body after it has travelled along a path that forms an oblique angle with the second body's point of impact or surface (e.g. squash ball hits the wall from an oblique angle) or *b)* the impact angle is oblique but both bodies are in motion prior to impact (e.g. cricket bat strikes the ball). Many of the impacts in sport involve different types of balls and implements and belong to the oblique category, but there are also impacts, which are not discussed here, involving more than two bodies coming into contact simultaneously (e.g. snooker balls).

To understand the mechanics of impacts and to be able to predict the post-impact events is very useful since these events dramatically affect the performance outcomes of many sporting situations. Some factors that influence the outcome of an impact were mentioned earlier but below there is a comprehensive list of factors that should be taken into account by sport scientists, coaches and athletes when attempting to understand and determine the outcome of a specific impact:

- the coefficient of restitution (e) of the impact, which depends on the degree of elasticity of both impacting bodies;
- the masses of the two impacting bodies;
- the velocity(ies) of the body(ies) before impact;
- the approach angle before impact;
- the type and the amount of spin (e.g. when one of the bodies is a spinning ball).

impacts

IMPACTS AND PERFORMANCE

The coefficient of restitution (e) is the ratio of the speed before impact to the speed after impact and is often expressed as a percentage. (A 100 per cent would indicate a perfect rebound, e.g. where a ball returns to the height from which it was dropped. Try this with a range of different sports balls and see what happens; you should see that even with really bouncy balls they do not return to the height they were dropped from.) The coefficient of restitution describes the elasticity of an impact (and not the elasticity of a body) and can be changed by altering the materials used to make the impacting bodies (e.g. different rubber compounds used in different grades of squash balls from beginner up to match balls). Other factors such as temperature will also affect the coefficient of restitution, which explains why squash balls get bouncier after they have been played with for a period of time. Scientific developments, especially with the introduction of new materials, have led to large performance improvements in sports that involve impacts (e.g. artificial surfaces in athletics and new tennis racquets).

Velocity, approach angle and spin are determined during the sports performance and are largely dependent on the performer's physical abilities and skills. However, factors related to the performer will also interact with environmental factors (e.g. temperature, humidity, wind direction and strength). The manipulation of performance variables within the constraints of the environmental factors to produce impacts that result in favourable outcomes is often what separates the performance of the more skilled individual from that of the less skilled.

IMPACTS AND INJURY

Many injuries that occur throughout sport are the result of different kinds of impacts. Single powerful impacts (e.g. head impacts from a fast delivery in cricket or from a stick in ice hockey) or repeated sizeable impacts (e.g. in running and jumping or in tennis) can lead to acute (e.g. head trauma) and chronic injuries (e.g. shin splints or tennis elbow) to the performer's body. The size of the forces experienced by the tissues during an impact is dependent on the product of the mass and deceleration of the striking object as it hits the body. Therefore, there is a tension between performance enhancement and the prevalence and incidence of injury related to impacts in sport. Both codes of rugby involve very large impacts between players which are quite legitimate within the rules of the game. However, in order to play rugby at the highest level, players need to be both highly skilled and well conditioned to both initiate successful impacts and withstand impacts initiated by other players, thereby affecting both their performance and the likelihood of becoming injured. The prevention and reduction of injuries due to impacts has received significant research attention over the recent decades and new technology has been engaged to control and improve outcomes of impacts. Protective equipment has been introduced or improved in many sports in an attempt to decrease the probability of certain injuries through impacts (e.g. helmets in cricket, gum shields, head guards and shoulder pads in rugby). In terms of single impacts the main purpose of the protective equipment, which is achieved by its unique shape and the elastic materials of its construction, is to absorb the energy of the impact and to spread the impact force over a larger area (e.g. cricket helmets, protective pads and gloves). With regard to repeated impacts, and especially those produced during running, jumping and landing, the focus has tended to be on modifying the impact-absorbing properties of the footwear rather than the compliance of the surfaces involved, since low compliance (high stiffness) of a surface can produce better performance in jumps and sprints due to the substantial amount of energy returned to the performer during the propulsive part of the ground contact. Running on more compliant surfaces would result in slower sprinting speeds, but there has been a compromise in the specification of modern athletic track surfaces, which have to conform to strict requirements in terms of mechanical properties such as compliance.

FURTHER READING

Hay, J.G. (1993) *The Biomechanics of Sports Techniques*, 4th edn. New Jersey: Prentice Hall. pp. 80–95.

Watkins, J. (2007) *Introduction to Biomechanics of Sport and Exercise*. Oxford: Elsevier Health Sciences.

Zatsiorsky, V. (2002) *Kinetics of Human Motion*. Champaign, IL: Human Kinetics.

NASSOS BISSAS
CARLTON COOKE

impacts

Work, Energy and Power

Forces are commonly applied over a certain distance. For example, a bobsleigh team will push their sleigh over a short distance in order to accelerate it. If a force is applied over a distance then a certain amount of work has been done. Work (Joules, J) is calculated by multiplying the magnitude of the force (Newtons, N) by the distance (metres, m) the body moves in the direction the force has moved it.

Power is a commonly used word whose meaning in biomechanics is the rate at which work is performed. It is often more important to be a powerful athlete, rather than just being 'strong'. The difference is that power is related to time, so if one particular weightlifter can lift 100 kg in two seconds, he is twice as powerful as another lifter who takes four seconds to lift the same mass. However, they could be considered equally strong as both have overcome the same resistance (and if both lift the bar the same distance, they will have completed the same amount of work). If we consider the equation for power constructed from above, we have:

$$\text{Power (Joules per second, J.s}^{-1}) = \text{work (J)/ time taken (s)}$$

or

$$\text{Power = force x displacement / time taken}$$

which can be rewritten as:

$$\text{Power (Watts, W) = force (N) x velocity (m.s}^{-1})$$

From the power equation above, it follows that how quickly an athlete moves a weight will depend on the resistive force it presents. If something has a resistance that cannot be overcome by the muscles' force, no velocity occurs and no power exists. Similarly, if no resistance is present, a large velocity occurs but once again there is negligible power because of the absence of force. In order to have a power output (and therefore to do work), force and velocity have to occur simultaneously. Individual muscles have their own optimum speed of movement to produce maximum power. As the velocity of movement increases from zero the power of the muscle increases rapidly until a plateau is reached. Further increases in the velocity will then result in a decrease in power output. If you think about pedalling on a bicycle, you will notice that using a low gear when travelling quickly has little or no effect on acceleration, because the forces applied are low and pedalling velocity is high. Likewise, pedalling in a high gear when cycling uphill is difficult because the resistive force is high in comparison to the speed of pedalling. It is therefore important in cycling that an appropriate gear is chosen to ensure maximum power output from the muscles, which is then applied through the pedals and chain to the back wheel.

Intertwined with force, work and power is the concept of energy. Energy is the capacity to do work. There are different kinds of energy and in each case they allow forces to act so that movement can occur. Similarly, in order to slow those movements (i.e. to decelerate), energy expenditure is also necessary.

Kinetic energy is the energy a body has as a result of its motion, and is dependent on both how heavy it is and how fast it's moving. A heavy rugby player running at eight metres per second has a much greater kinetic energy than a light distance runner moving at five metres per second. As a result, it is much harder to stop the rugby player because more energy (in the opposite direction of movement) is required to decelerate the player.

Potential energy is the energy a body has as a result of its height above the ground and its weight. Weight is the force due to gravity acting on a given mass, and the higher an object or person is above the ground, the longer gravity has to accelerate the body during flight. Potential energy and kinetic energy are thus interrelated when a body is in flight. For example, a tennis ball thrown high into the air will have a relatively high kinetic energy to begin with, but this will reduce as it gains height due to the slowing action of gravity. However, the potential energy of the ball is continually increasing until the peak of its flight when it is at its maximum. In this case, kinetic energy is being converted to potential energy. When the ball starts to fall back to earth, gaining speed (and therefore gaining kinetic energy), it simultaneously loses height and therefore potential energy. Potential energy is being converted back to kinetic energy, and this is one example of the physical law of the conservation of energy, which states that energy cannot be made or destroyed but only converted from one form to another.

The main forms of chemical energy for fuelling sports movement in humans come from glycogen stored in the muscles and liver and fat stored in the muscle and elsewhere in the body. These fuels are sources of chemical energy that are converted to kinetic energy (movement of muscles) and heat energy. In fact, the majority of chemical energy provided from food is heat energy and relatively little is used mechanically by the muscles during contraction to produce movement. The body can therefore be described as being relatively inefficient. Efficiency is a measure of how much energy is wasted by a particular process (% Efficiency = Output Energy/Input Energy × 100). For the purposes of movement, much heat energy is wasted energy because it does not help sports performance beyond a certain point. In fact, the body has to then work hard to dissipate this heat, which can have a severe detrimental effect on performance; this is achieved through various methods, but the main mechanism is sweating.

In motor sport, the engineers and designers continually strive to maximise the efficiency of the vehicle. Formula One cars are especially designed to reduce slowing forces such as air resistance because the more forces needing to be overcome, the more energy is required. Energy requirements need to be kept down so that the car can carry less fuel (which adds weight) and require less refuelling stops. Be careful not to confuse efficiency with economy, as economy refers to how well the system uses the fuels it draws on. In a car this might mean how well the petrol or diesel is burned in the engine, in the human body it refers to how much oxygen is utilised to produce a certain exercise intensity (e.g. run at a given speed).

FURTHER READING

Bartlett, R. (2002) *Introduction to Sports Biomechanics*. London: Taylor & Francis.
Hamill, J. and Knutzen, K.M. (2003) *Biomechanical Basis of Human Movement*, 2nd edn. Philadelphia, PA: Lippincott, Williams & Wilkins.
Watkins, J. (2007) *Introduction to Biomechanics of Sport and Exercise*. Oxford: Elsevier Health Sciences.

BRIAN HANLEY

Angular Kinetics

Angular kinetics has similar concepts to those of linear kinetics, such as force, **Work, Energy and Power**, although they are somewhat more complicated. The important concepts in angular kinetics are levers, torque and angular momentum.

LEVERS

A lever is defined as a rigid body that rotates about an axis, which is also sometimes called a fulcrum or a pivot. Levers rotate about an axis due to a force being applied, generally to overcome a resistance. In the human body, the bones are the main levers, the joints are the axes, the muscles provide the force by contracting, and the weight of the body segment (with or without an extra implement or weight) is the resistance.

First-class levers are useful if a large resistance has to be overcome with a small force. First-class levers occur when the axis is placed between the force and the resistance (it is easiest to picture this as a see-saw). Opening a tin of paint with a screwdriver is a common application of this type of lever. First-class levers are also helpful for moving small resistances quickly. An example in the human body is the triceps brachii in the upper arm. The force of the muscle causes rotation around the elbow axis so that the resistance of the forearm is overcome.

Second-class levers are useful to move large resistances with little force. Second-class levers have the resistance located between the force and the axis. A good example of this type of lever is a wheelbarrow. There are very few meaningful examples of this type of lever in the human body, because it is mostly built for speed of movement. One example is standing up on your toes, where the fulcrum is your metatarsal-phalanges joints (ball of the foot), the resistance is the weight of the body and the force is supplied by the calf muscles. The human body mainly consists of third-class levers, which occur when the force is placed between the resistance and the axis. One example is elbow flexion. The force is provided predominantly by the biceps brachii, the axis is the elbow joint, and the resistance is provided by the forearm. Note how the biceps brachii is a third-class lever while the triceps brachii is a first-class lever because of the different positioning of their tendinous insertions.

How well a lever works depends on the length of the lever and the positions of the force and resistance from its axis. The distance from the axis to the point of force application is called the force arm, while the distance from the axis to the point of resistance application is called the resistance arm. Multiplying the force arm length (m) by the force (N) applied gives a turning moment (Nm), sometimes known as a torque. In order for the lever to be effective, the 'effort' torque has to be greater than the resisting torque (calculated in the same manner as the 'effort' torque).

The longer the force arm, the less force is required to overcome the resistance; and the shorter the resistance arm, the less force is required also. It is rare in the human body to have long force arms and short resistance arms. It is usually the opposite in that the resistances are a much greater distance from the joints than where the forces are applied (i.e. muscular insertions). This situation is known as a mechanical disadvantage. A mechanical advantage occurs when the effort force arm is longer than the resistance arm and this occurs in some first-class levers and all second-class levers.

TORQUE, MOMENT OF INERTIA AND RADIUS OF GYRATION

Torque is the angular version of force. Similarly to force, a torque is something that causes angular acceleration. A rotating object will rotate more quickly, more slowly or change direction if a torque is applied. How effective the torque is does not just depend on how heavy the rotating object is but also on how that weight is distributed with respect to the axis of rotation. This resistive property of rotating bodies is known as the moment of inertia, and the distance from the axis to where the moment of inertia is said to act is known as the radius of gyration. It is worth pointing out that the point where the moment of inertia is said to act is not always the centre of mass. For example, a discus in flight will rotate around its centre of mass but will still have a certain resistance to rotation because its moment of inertia is slightly further out on the discus.

The radius of gyration is of great importance in altering how fast rotation occurs. This is because changing the radius of gyration changes the moment of inertia and hence the resistance to rotation. So if the radius of gyration is shortened, the resistance to rotation is decreased and positive angular acceleration occurs. In effect, the rotating body's angular velocity increases. For example, a baseball bat swings faster if it is held further up the bat than normal – this technique is often adpoted by children for whom the bat is often too long and heavy to swing successfully.

A sprinter's leg during the swing phase of running is also a rotating body, and can be made to complete the running step more quickly by reducing the leg's radius of gyration. This is achieved through maximal flexing at the knee, bringing all the leg's mass closer to the hip joint. In some sporting situations, it is preferable to reduce angular velocity and this is achieved through increasing the radius of gyration. One example is the sail technique in long jumping, where the athletes spreads out their arms to prevent forward rotation. Among other things, this prevents the athlete from somersaulting, a technique forbidden in the event.

CONSERVATION OF ANGULAR MOMENTUM

We have seen that there is a relationship between angular velocity and moment of inertia. If we multiply the moment of inertia by angular velocity, we can calculate angular momentum, which is defined as the quantity of angular motion. By decreasing the moment of inertia, angular velocity increases, and vice versa. This is the principle of conservation of angular momentum, and applies to all bodies rotating in the air (it is normally assumed that in this situation there is negligible air resistance). It is this principle that allows gymnasts and divers to control the speed of their rotations when tucking or piking. A diver might tuck during flight to spin quickly during forward somersaults and then open out again towards the bottom of flight in order to enter the water with a straight body.

FURTHER READING

Kreighbaum, E. and Barthels, K.M. (1996) *Biomechanics: A Qualitative Approach for Studying Human Movement*, 4th edn. Minneapolis, MN: Burgess Publishing Company.
Watkins, J. (2007) *Introduction to Biomechanics of Sport and Exercise*. Oxford: Elsevier Health Sciences.
Zatsiorsky, V. (2002) *Kinetics of Human Motion*. Champaign, IL: Human Kinetics.

BRIAN HANLEY

angular kinetics

A projectile is an object that is moving through the air unassisted with only gravity and air resistance acting upon it. There are numerous examples of projectiles in sport including sports objects such as a golf ball, basketball, tennis ball, rugby ball, football, shuttlecock, discus, hammer and frisbee, and sports performers such as long jumpers, high jumpers, gymnasts, figure skaters, ski-jumpers and sky divers. Projectile motion refers to the type of motion experienced by projectiles travelling through air and, ignoring air resistance, is a special example of linear **Kinematics** where we know what changes in velocity and acceleration there will be once an object or body is released. Ignoring air resistance is okay in a number of sports examples (e.g. shot putt) where the effects are so small that they can really be ignored. In contrast, air resistance is crucial in sky-diving as the difference between hitting the ground with and without an open parachute is generally the difference between life and death! In sport-related examples of projectile motion we need to be aware of the different aims of different sports. In **Biomechanics** we refer to primary mechanical purpose as the key purpose of the sport. In long jump this is projecting the body for maximum horizontal displacement; in high jump it is projecting the body for maximum vertical displacement. These two events require different approaches to the point of projection due to the difference in primary mechanical purpose.

GRAVITY AND PARABOLIC FLIGHT

If we continue to ignore air resistance, then in projectile motion the only force acting on the object or body is due to gravity, which we experience because of the huge mass of the earth attracting our mass or the mass of objects that we throw or project in sport. Gravity is the force of attraction between two objects of different mass and the different size of the earth and our moon explains why gravity is about nine times less on the moon. The acceleration due to gravity on the surface of the earth (at sea level) is approximately 9.81 m.s^{-2} and is accelerating any projectile during the whole of its flight, meaning that the vertical velocity (gravity acts vertically down towards the centre of the earth) is increasing by 9.81 m.s^{-1} every second. Many people find this confusing because when you throw a ball up in the air it immediately slows down, achieving zero velocity at the top of its flight before accelerating to the same speed when it drops back down to the same height at which it was released. This is an example of where the difference between vector and scalar quantities is important (acceleration is a vector quantity so has both magnitude and direction, in the case of gravity on earth 9.81 m.s^{-2} acting vertically downwards). So, ignoring air resistance, we can simplify projectile motion to a consideration of constant acceleration due to gravity (9.81 m.s^{-2}) because if we ignore air resistance there is zero horizontal acceleration, which means that the horizontal velocity does not change throughout the flight of the object or body. So a shot will be travelling at the same horizontal velocity at the point of release as it is on landing as we can ignore air resistance in that event. This means that, if we know the conditions at release of the object or body (i.e. its velocity, both magnitude and direction are necessary), then, ignoring air resistance, we can easily assess the projectile motion of the object or body.

The flight path of a projectile is called its trajectory. In the case of either a high jumper as soon as they leave the ground, or when a cricketer throwing the ball in from the boundary lets go, this is known in both cases as the instant (referring to time) or point of release (referring to position). Once the high jumper or ball is in flight, gravity is continually causing the body or object to experience the constant acceleration of 9.81 m.s^{-2}. Ignoring air resistance and given that the velocity at release was not vertical (i.e. less than 90° to the horizontal) means that the object or body will then follow a trajectory or flight path that will describe a symmetrical curve, with the line of symmetry acting vertically through the point of maximum height. This curve is known as a parabola and is why in mechanics the projectile motion of an object or body may be referred to as parabolic (Figure 1). If the object or body is projected vertically it will go straight up until it reaches zero velocity and then accelerate due to gravity until it reaches the same magnitude of velocity but in the opposite direction. It is worth remembering that we ignore the effects of air resistance both horizontally and vertically to produce the parabolic trajectory.

FACTORS AFFECTING PROJECTILE MOTION

There are three main factors that affect the trajectory of an object or body in flight: the projection angle, magnitude of projection velocity and height of projection.

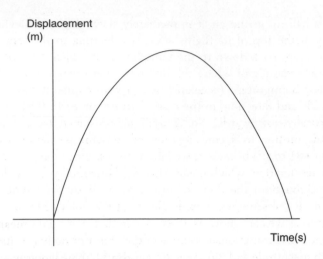

Figure 1.1 *A parabolic trajectory or flight path for an object or body as it travels through the air (ignoring effects of air resistance)*

Projection angle

The projection angle, i.e. the angle between the initial trajectory and the horizontal, determines the shape of the parabola described in flight by the object or body. Projection angles in some sports can be negative, such as downhill shots off cliff tops or hills in golf, in ski-jumping, or when performing a tennis serve. More generally they are between 0 and 90° to the horizontal and as a consequence will produce a parabolic shape as shown in Figure 1, but the steepness or shallowness of the curve will depend on the angle of projection, with angles greater than 45° producing steeper curves and angles less than 45° producing shallower curves.

Ignoring air resistance and with the point of release at the same height as the point of landing the optimum angle for maximum horizontal distance of flight is 45°, but there are factors in sport which mean that 45° is rarely the optimum for maximum horizontal distance. As mentioned previously, the primary mechanical purpose will affect the optimum angle of projection. In high jump the optimum angle is in the range of 40 to 48°, where the primary mechanical purpose is maximum vertical height. In contrast, in long jump, where the primary mechanical purpose is maximum horizontal distance, the take off angles are in the range of 18–27°.

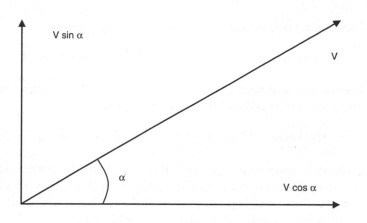

Figure 2 *Measuring projection velocity magnitude*

Magnitude of projection velocity

For a given angle of projection the magnitude of the velocity at release will determine both the height and the horizontal distance of the trajectory of the object or body. Initial conditions for projectiles are therefore normally summarised by the measurement of the angle of projection (α) and the magnitude of the velocity (V), the two components of the vector quantity which is the resultant projection velocity (Figure 2).

The initial conditions for projection are defined by the projection velocity resultant vector, having magnitude V and direction specified by α. The vertical component is given by V sin α and the horizontal component by V cos α.

The vertical and horizontal component vectors (Figure 2) derived from the resultant projection velocity vector are important and should be considered separately as they define the height and the horizontal distance of the trajectory, all other things remaining equal. After release the vertical velocity V sin α is reduced by the effects of gravity by 9.81 m.s^{-1} for every second of vertical flight time. Vertical velocity will therefore reduce due to the constant acceleration due to gravity of 9.81 m.s^{-2}, which is acting vertically downwards towards the centre of the earth, causing a deceleration. This reduction will continue until zero velocity at the top of the flight trajectory, which is sometimes referred to as the apex of the trajectory, after which it will accelerate at 9.81 m.s^{-2}, gaining velocity as it now falls back towards the earth's centre.

The time it takes to get to zero vertical velocity is given by:

$$\text{Time to apex} = \text{vertical velocity/gravity} = V \sin \alpha/9.81 \text{ m.s}^{-2}$$

If the object or body lands at the same height it was projected from then the total flight time is double the time to the apex:

$$\text{Flight time} = 2 \times (V \sin \alpha/9.81 \text{ m.s}^{-2}) \text{ or } 2 \times (V \sin \alpha/g)$$

In contrast, because we are ignoring air resistance, the horizontal velocity $V \cos \alpha$ remains constant throughout flight. Since we know that displacement = velocity × time, the horizontal displacement of the projectile when it lands, called the range, will be given by:

$$\text{Range} = V \cos \alpha \times (2 \times V \sin \alpha/g) = (2 \ V^2 \sin \alpha \cos \alpha)/g$$

$$\text{Range} = (V^2 \sin 2\alpha)/g \text{ (because } 2 \sin \alpha \cos \alpha = \sin 2\alpha)$$

$$\text{Maximum range} = \text{maximum value of } (V^2 \sin 2\alpha)/g$$

$$\text{Maximum value of } \sin 2\alpha \text{ is } \sin 90° = 1, \text{ therefore}$$
$$\alpha = 45° \text{ and}$$

$$\text{Maximum range} = V^2/g$$

Therefore, the theoretical maximum range for projecting an object or body on a horizontal surface is produced by a projection angle of 45°, as mentioned before.

Because projectiles are an example of uniform acceleration due to gravity, the regular equations for uniform acceleration can be used to calculate variables in projectile motion. These equations are:

$$v = u + at, \ s = ut + \tfrac{1}{2} at^2 \text{ and } v^2 = u^2 + 2as$$

where v = final velocity (m.s^{-1}), u = initial velocity (m.s^{-1}), a = acceleration (m.s^{-2}), t = time (s).

Height of projection

The third factor that affects the trajectory of a projectile in sport is the height of the point of projection or release in relation to the landing surface of the object or body. There are examples from sport where the height of projection is both above and below the landing surface. For example in the shot putt the optimum angle is less than 45° because the point of release is well above the surface on which it lands (more than 2 m higher in senior male shot putters). In hitting a golf ball up a slope the optimum angle of projection will be greater than 45°, a ball struck at 45° will simply hit the uphill slope prematurely. In contrast, a tennis serve is hit as an attacking shot down from the point of release from the racquet head into the service court on the other side of the net, so the angle of projection here ranges typically from −3 to −15°.

AIR RESISTANCE

Everything discussed so far has ignored air resistance, but there are many examples where we use air resistance to great effect in sport when projecting objects or bodies, such as a discus and a ski-jumper (see **Fluid Mechanics**).

FURTHER READING

Bartlett, R. (2002) *Introduction to Sports Biomechanics*. London: Taylor & Francis.
Kreighbaum, E. and Barthels, K.M. (1996) *Biomechanics: A Qualitative Approach for Studying Human Movement*, 4th edn. Minneapolis, MN: Burgess Publishing Company.
Watkins, J. (2007) *Introduction to Biomechanics of Sport and Exercise*. Oxford: Elsevier Health Sciences.

CARLTON COOKE
CHRISTOPHER LOW

fluid mechanics

Fluid Mechanics

Fluid mechanics is the area of sport and exercise biomechanics that helps us understand the forces exerted on objects or bodies by interactions with the fluid they are travelling through. These are often studied separately where the fluid is air (aerodynamics) or water (hydrodynamics).

However, the two main concepts and mechanical principles are the same for both:

- drag forces, which are forces that are parallel and opposite to the motion of the object or body as it moves through a fluid, and
- lift forces, which always act perpendicular (at a right angle (90°)) to the direction of flow of the fluid.

To understand drag and lift forces we must focus on the relative motion between the object or body and the fluid that it is moving through. The importance of this principle is illustrated by ski-jumpers, who in optimum conditions when jumping into an oncoming breeze, can generate lift forces that carry them considerably further than they would jump without the oncoming wind. However, cross-winds interfere with the technique of ski-jumping and often mean that competitions have to be postponed until there are more favourable wind conditions. In the case of the relative motion of air flow and the ski-jumper:

- in still conditions the ski-jumper will only experience air flow past their skis and body in the direction opposite to their travel;
- jumping into an oncoming wind will increase the flow of air past their skis and body, due to their velocity added to the velocity of the wind which is blowing towards them;
- in a cross-wind the ski-jumper will experience a flow of air that will be the combination (resultant vector) of the velocity of the cross-wind and the velocity of their movement through the air as a result of their jump, making it impossible to jump straight down the fall line of the hill.

DRAG FORCES

A drag force is a fluid resistance force that opposes the motion of an object or body moving through it and is called either aerodynamic or hydrodynamic drag respectively. A good example of a large difference in drag force when moving in air is given by a comparison of cycling with dropped handle bars in a crouched racing position and straight handle bars with the rider in an upright position. The same cyclist going at the same speed will experience very different drag forces in the two different body positions. Similarly, in swimming the position of the body in the water will have a large effect on the drag forces. A streamlined position with the whole body on or close to the surface of the water will create much less drag than in a swimmer who allows their legs to sink, which increases the drag forces. Both these examples of different drag forces in air and water are explained almost completely by body position in relation to the oncoming fluid, be it air or water. However, there are several other important variables that contribute to drag forces.

Skin friction and profile drag are common to both air and water and a third form of drag that is important in water sports is wave drag. Skin friction or surface drag is caused by the fluid in contact with the body or object moving with the surface of the object against the flow, which drags along the fluid next to it, but this effect decreases with increasing distance away from the body or object. This rubbing of layers of fluid causes friction and is known as the boundary layer. Skin friction, which is the interaction between the body or object and the fluid layers, depends on the roughness of the surface and the viscosity of the fluid. Profile, pressure or form drag refer to the drag caused by the pressure difference between the zone of high pressure on the front of the body or object as it moves through the air and the low pressure zone behind the object. These different pressure zones are caused where the boundary layer of fluid flowing around the body or object breaks away from it, as the fluid cannot flow smoothly all the way around the surface of the object, which causes a low pressure turbulent zone behind the object. The pressure difference between the high and low pressure zones causes a net profile drag force on the body or object, which is the largest air resistance variable that affects athletes moving quickly, such as runners and speed skaters and all projectiles in sport, such as balls or javelins. Both skin friction and profile drag depend on shape, size and position of the object or body, the density of the fluid (water is denser than air) and the velocity of the fluid flow relative to the object or body. Wave drag is the resistance force caused by a body moving along, through or under the surface of the water that produces waves. At low speeds wave drag is not that significant, but it can become the largest resistance force at high speeds. Front-crawl swimmers do make use of the trough of the bow wave to make breathing easier. Wave drag in rowing boats, kayaks and canoes is related to boat length, with a longer boat length facilitating higher possible boat speeds.

Drag force is based on the following equation:

$$\text{Drag force} = \tfrac{1}{2}\,\text{coefficient of drag} \times \text{frontal area} \times \text{fluid density} \times \text{relative flow velocity}^2$$

$$F_D = \tfrac{1}{2}\,C_D\,A\,\rho v^2$$

Where F_D is the drag force, C_D is the coefficient of drag, A is the frontal area perpendicular to the flow, ρ is the fluid density and v is the velocity.

The coefficient of drag, which tells us how streamlined a body or object is, changes with the position of the body or object relative to the flow and is determined experimentally. Streamlining depends not only on shape but also on orientation to the direction of fluid flow, so you can have a streamlined shape, such as a javelin, which stalls because it is not correctly orientated to the flow of oncoming air. Frontal area is the area of the body or object facing the flow of fluid, as illustrated above in the example of body position in cycling. Fluid density (mass/volume) represents how closely the atoms of the fluid are arranged, with air being almost 1,000 times less dense than water. The density of air will vary with humidity, temperature and pressure and changes in the density of air from the height of a delivery from the hand of a bowler in cricket to the level of the pitch contribute to how much the ball will move in the air. Such effects will vary depending on the environmental conditions, which is why a swing bowler's performance will vary with the weather conditions. As shown by the equation, drag force increases with the square of the velocity, so the effects of a given coefficient of drag and frontal area on the drag forces are magnified by an increase in the relative flow velocity.

Drag forces as propulsion

Although drag forces oppose the motion of an object or body, they are not always negative in their contribution to the sport or exercise. This is well illustrated by the example of a sky diver who opens their parachute, which dramatically increases the drag force, slowing them down sufficiently so they can execute a safe landing. Another example is the drag force exerted on the blade of an oar in rowing as it is pulled backwards through the water, which is responsible for propelling the boat forward.

LIFT FORCES

Lift forces are most commonly explained with reference to the pressure differences created by different speeds of air travelling either side of an aerofoil or hydrofoil. Figure 3 shows a cross-section of an aerofoil, which could be an aircraft wing. The explanation is that air dividing at the front edge of the aerofoil travels faster over the longer curved surface of the top of the aerofoil compared with the air flowing underneath the straight surface of the bottom of the aerofoil. These different speeds of air flow relative to the surface of the aerofoil develop different pressures, with high pressure developed underneath the aerofoil, where the

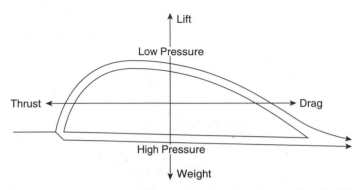

Figure 3   *Forces acting on an aerofoil (this way up it could be the wing of an aircraft, upside down it could be an aerofoil on a racing car with the 'lift' force pushing the car into the track)*

flow velocity is slow and low pressure above the aerofoil where the flow velocity is fast. The lift force is therefore the result of the pressure difference between the top and bottom of the aerofoil, which results in the aerofoil experiencing a lift force in the direction from high to low pressure perpendicular to the relative flow of the fluid and directly proportional to the magnitude of pressure difference.

The relationship between pressure and flow velocity is summarised by Bernoulli's principle, which states the inverse relationship, when the flow of fluid is fast the pressure is low and when the flow velocity is slow the pressure is high. You can demonstrate this principle easily by taking two sheets of A4 paper, one in each hand and holding them in front of your mouth about 10 cm apart, supporting each in the middle of the long side so that they hang down parallel making a channel in front of your mouth. Blow air down the channel between the two pieces of paper and observe what happens. The two pieces move together because the flow velocity in the channel is relatively fast as you blow the air through compared to the air on the outside of the paper, which is still. This generates a low pressure zone in the channel with a lift force acting horizontally forcing the two pieces of paper together in the channel. Another two important observations to make are that you do not need an aerofoil shape to generate pressure differences and lift forces, and that lift forces can act in any direction (not just up!) according to where the different pressure zones are. The aerofoil shown in Figure 3 illustrates how lift forces are generated to help keep planes in the air, or the hulls of hydrofoils out of the water (although you need a lot of

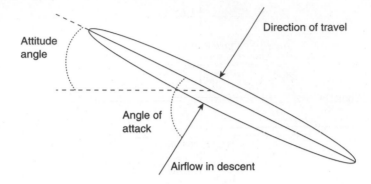

Figure 4 *Angle of attack of a discus during the descent phase of the throw*

forward speed to generate big enough lift forces in both cases). However, if you turn the aerofoil over (or turn the book upside down) you will be looking at how an aerofoil helps keeps a Formula One racing car on the track (again the faster it goes the faster the relative air flow, the greater the pressure difference and the more lift force is generated).

Angle of Attack

If a body or object does not have an aerofoil shape, a difference in flow velocity can be created to generate a lift force resulting from differences in pressure by tilting the body or object relative to the oncoming fluid flow. This angle of tilt between the oncoming fluid and the body or object is called the angle of attack. A good example from sport is the discus throw, where at the point of release the thrower releases the discus with a negative angle of attack in order to benefit from relatively large lift forces in the descending part of the flight path of the discus (Figure 4). This is achieved because the discus tends to maintain the same angle between its axis and the ground (attitude angle) throughout its flight, which is helped by the gyroscopic stability generated by the spinning of the discus at release. Good discus throwers therefore throw better into a light wind because they can generate greater lift forces. Poor discus throwers often get the angle of attack wrong at release, which means it will be wrong throughout the throw and stall, falling steeply for a shorter throw in the descent part of flight. Some biomechanists adopt an alternative approach to explaining the use of angle of attack through Newton's laws of motion.

Factors that cause lift

The magnitude of lift force that can be generated is dependent on a number of factors, which can be summarised by the following equation:

Lift force = ½ coefficient of lift × pressure area × fluid density × relative flow velocity^2

$$F_L = \tfrac{1}{2} \, C_L \, A \, \rho v^2$$

where F_L is the lift force, C_L is the coefficient of lift, A is the pressure area which is the surface area of the body where the pressure acts, ρ is the fluid density and v is the velocity.

The coefficient of lift is the index of how well an object can generate lift force, but will be different depending on its orientation to the flow of fluid (i.e. dependent on angle of attack). Using the discus throw as an example, an angle of attack of approximately 26° will produce a higher coefficient of lift than for larger or smaller angles of attack, but this angle will vary throughout the flight of the discus.

The size of the surface area that is angled to the flow, which generates the pressure differences, is positively related to the generation of lift forces. Design features of objects used in sport are often manipulated in order to generate lift in this way, which is why rules are often introduced to control such factors. For example, single design sailing boats will focus on testing the skill of the sailors when they race, although how the sails are rigged and set for the prevailing conditions will affect how well the boat performs.

The density of fluid is also positively related to the generation of lift forces, with water generating more lift than air. This is similar to the effect of density on drag forces.

Also similar to the effects on drag, lift forces will increase with the square of the relative velocity between the fluid and the object. This means that if the velocity doubles the lift force generated will increase by a factor of four.

FURTHER READING

Kreighbaum, E. and Barthels, K.M. (1996) *Biomechanics: A Qualitative Approach for Studying Human Movement*, 4th edn. Minneapolis, MN: Burgess Publishing Company.

MacGinnis, P.M. (2005) *Biomechanics of Sport and Exercise*, 2nd edn. Champaign, IL: Human Kinetics.

CARLTON COOKEG

PART II

Exercise Physiology

INTRODUCTION

Physiology is concerned with the study of how the body works (*physio* meaning 'nature' and *ology* meaning 'the study of'). It is complemented by the study of anatomy, which is concerned with the structure of the body. The term complementarity refers to how structure informs function when studying how the body works. Exercise physiology is a subdiscipline of physiology, which is the focus of this section of the book, and is concerned with the study of the effects of muscular activity in the form of physical activity, exercise or sport on the structure and function of the human body. Exercise physiology is based on the early science of Greece and Asia Minor, with the contributions of the Greek physicians, Herodicus, Hippocrates and Galen acknowledged as having the greatest influence on western civilisation.

One useful way to help consider how the body works is to begin with an understanding of the structural organisation of the human body. Six levels of organisation are relevant to understanding how the body works, progressing from the smallest to the largest: chemical, cellular, tissue, organ, system and organism.

The chemical level includes atoms, which are the smallest units of matter that form the basis of chemical reactions and molecules, that are two or more atoms joined together. Molecules are combined to form cells, which are the basic building blocks of structure and function within the human body. Tissues are groups of cells that work together to produce a particular function. The four basic types of tissue within the body are: epithelial, connective, muscular and nervous. Epithelial tissue is the lining and cover for body surfaces, hollow organs, cavities and ducts and it also forms glands. Connective tissue protects and supports the body and its organs. Muscle tissue, crucial in all forms of physical activity, generates the forces that are exerted on the bones of the skeletal system to make the body structures move. Nervous tissue detects change both inside and outside the body and generates nerve impulses that help maintain bodily function and **Homeostasis**, which is explained in a separate entry. Organs comprise different types of tissue that are joined together and have specific functions and are usually recognisable from their shape, such as the heart or lungs.

Systems consist of organs that are related to each other and have a common function. An example of a system that is relevant in all aspects of exercise physiology is the muscular system, which is made up of skeletal, smooth and cardiac muscle. Skeletal muscles get their name because they are normally attached to bones that are part of the skeletal system. It is the combined action of different muscles and the forces they exert on the bones that causes movement that we describe as either physical activity or exercise. Muscle contraction is initiated by the nervous system, which generates action potentials in the form of nerve impulses from the brain and spinal cord that stimulate the muscles to contract.

Eleven systems work together in the human body: cardiovascular, digestive, endocrine, integumentary, lymphatic and immune, muscular, nervous, reproductive, respiratory, skeletal and urinary systems. The organism that we are concerned with in human exercise physiology, which is the largest of the six organisation levels, is the human body and comprises all the parts of the body functioning together.

You can gain a good understanding of exercise physiology by learning about the basic structure and function of the human body from first principles, using the components of the organisational structure outlined above. Another instructive way to inform your understanding of the application of exercise physiology is to take a concept or example of physical activity or exercise that is relevant to your specific interests and use that to provide a focus for studying how exercise physiology contributes to explaining how the body works and responds. One advantage of this approach is that you will integrate your learning, covering different systems and organisational levels of the body as you begin to understand how they interact to explain how the body works in different settings and responds to different stimuli provided by different types of physical activity and exercise, or indeed a lack of it.

This section of the book presents entries introducing the key components of exercise physiology, from important systems, such as the muscular and **Energy Systems**, to the processes of homeostasis, concepts of fitness and **Principles of Training**. **Nutrition** and **Biochemistry** are disciplines or areas of study in their own right. However, they are often introduced within the study of exercise physiology at the beginning of undergraduate sport and exercise science courses, so are included here in separate entries.

CARLTON COOKE

Nutrition and Biochemistry

Reductionism has driven the subject matter of both biochemistry and nutrition to the level of the molecule, its interactions in the widest sense and its metabolic fate. The idea that a true understanding of the basic components of the system, in this case the chemical substances, themselves can explain life itself underpins the approach but it is realised that emergence, the properties of systems is also of importance. While biochemistry sets out to explain the complex interrelationships of molecules in terms of metabolism, metabolic pathways and regulation *in* living systems, nutrition aims to elucidate the intake and assimilation of food and how these nutrients are absorbed, digested, converted and used *by* the body. An understanding of both biochemistry and nutrition is therefore crucial when studying sport and exercise science either from the perspective of sports performance or that of physical activity and health.

MOLECULAR FUNCTION

Molecular identity is determined by the arrangement of elements (such as carbon, hydrogen, oxygen and nitrogen) and the precise linkage of these by chemical bonds, this being unique for a given substance and in turn determining a three-dimensional form that is associated with highly specific properties (exploited by evolution as function). The very combination of individual elements results in such diverse molecular behaviour determined by the structure and bonding of the molecule itself such that:

- molecules like water (H_2O) are able to solvate other substances;
- adenosine triphosphate (ATP) has exploitable and usable high bond energy;
- lysolecithin, a phospholipid, is polar and can be utilised in membrane barrier structure to separate different cell compartments; whereas
- enzymes (giant molecules comprised of a variety of amino acids) can act as biological catalysts.

METABOLISM

Many of the molecules associated with life are organic molecules (i.e. they contain carbon) but the interaction of all these substances usually occurs in aqueous solution. The complexities of an organism may be reduced to the operation and regulation of metabolic pathways through which flow those molecules acquired as a result of nutrition. Thus glucose, a carbohydrate $C_6H_{12}O_6$ may be eaten as starch, a nutrient found in potato, but once assimilated within the body, the molecule of glucose may pass through a variety of metabolic pathways undergoing chemical transformations controlled by a succession of linked organic reactions catalysed by distinct sets of enzymes to either be used for energy (oxidation, the glucose ultimately producing CO_2), storage (glycogen or fat) or inter-conversion to another molecule (e.g. galactose).

Metabolic pathways may be catabolic (energy-producing) or anabolic (energy-consuming), the control of which determines growth, reproduction and all that constitutes the maintenance of life. A feature of metabolism is **Homeostasis** (see separate entry) whereby, despite wide fluctuations in external conditions, the internal environment of the cell and organism is maintained within tolerable limits. Thus metabolic pathways exist as discrete sets of chemical reactions in an apparent constant condition, but in reality movement of material or flux through the pathways are under constant dynamic adjustment of equilibrium.

A living body is a self-assembling, self-regulating automatic system of organic molecules operating with maximum economy of components and pathways. These metabolic reactions have evolved for the transfer of energy and for the production of its own components and are possible under ambient conditions because of the enzymes synthesised by itself. Collections of metabolic pathways are linked, integrated and controlled such that a given cell is a viable entity, yet collections of cells (tissues), grouped tissues (organs) and organ systems constitute a fully functional organism. This is achieved through hierarchical control exerted from the level of the enzyme (e.g. allosteric control), control of physiological variables such as fluid osmolality, often by hormones (e.g. kidney and anti-diuretic hormone (ADH)) through to powerful homeostatic controls exerted through neuro-endocrine networks impacting on the whole system (e.g. growth hormone). Yet at the heart of this system heredity control lies with DNA and RNA in the cell nucleus. Chromosome gene expression by transcription and translation is responsible for the set of gene products and enzymes unique to a given organism to sustain life.

Understanding metabolism is important in terms of both sports performance and physical activity and health. For example, an understanding of the metabolic pathways that are responsible for the provision of ATP, which is the energy currency of the body, can help with the design of appropriate training programmes for different sports that make very different demands on our metabolism. Metabolic responses and adaptations to a physically active or sedentary lifestyle are key components in defining disease risk and state for a range of lifestyle-related and therefore largely preventable diseases such as metabolic syndrome, obesity, type 2 diabetes and coronary heart disease.

NUTRITION

Nutrition provides the molecules necessary to sustain life; metabolism provides the mechanism necessary to exploit these to derive building blocks for synthesis of organism-specific material. The fabric of an organism is forever undergoing change because there is a fine balance between the rate at which new materials replace components that are either time-expired through natural metabolic breakdown and synthesis (e.g. protein turnover) or have been expended to supply energy by oxidation (e.g. glycogen). Nutrition then is the constant need to provide the organism with components to maintain the status quo, but especially its protein and energy balance. Food furnishes the fuels and substrates of the right sort in the form of carbohydrates, lipids and protein that by the process of metabolism yield the necessary intermediates from which the composition of the body is maintained. Such macronutrients are acquired, together with micronutrients such as vitamins and minerals along with water, to constitute a diet that provides our well-evolved and highly developed systems with the capacity for anabolic (synthesis) and catabolic (breakdown) reactions, not only to sustain life but to sustain growth and reproduction. In this way the delicate structure of membranes, the ultrastructure of the cells and the complete integrity of the organism are maintained but only operate at the cost of continual expenditure of energy and an essential need for the supply of new components through adequate nutrition.

Understanding nutrition is therefore important for both the perspectives of physical activity and health and sports performance. In the same way that design, production, fine-tuning and practice are necessary to produce a winning Formula One race car, such a car will only perform at its best if the correct fuel is used and supplied at the right time and rate. This analogy explains why an understanding of metabolism and nutrition are critical to sports scientists, coaches and performers in getting the most out of the fuel supplied through an appropriately designed diet to either achieve objectives in high-performance sport or to benefit health alongside physical activity in everyday life.

KEY POINTS

- Biochemistry is the study of chemical processes and their control in living organisms.
- Nutrition is the study of the acquisition, utilisation and composition of food, the way in which food is metabolised and converted for use by the body and the need for specific and identifiable nutrient components that support life.
- Metabolism constitutes all the chemical reactions associated with life and is highly dependent upon enzymes operating as biological catalysts in tightly ordered and controlled sets of interconnected pathways through which organic material flows.
- Biochemistry and nutrition are essential for understanding how to produce excellence in sport or to live a healthy balanced lifestyle.

FURTHER READING

Houston, M.E. (2006) *Biochemistry Primer for Exercise Science*, 3rd edn. Champaign, IL: Human Kinetics.

The Nutrition Society (2003) *Nutrition and Metabolism*, M.J. Gibney, I.A. Macdonald and H.M. Roche (eds). Oxford: Blackwell.

ROD KING
LOUISE SUTTON

key concepts in
sport & exercise sciences

Homeostasis

WHY SHOULD A SPORTS AND EXERCISE SCIENTIST BE INTERESTED IN HOMEOSTASIS?

Three of the major homeostatic mechanisms that are particularly relevant to sport and exercise are: thermoregulation, osmoregulation and regulation of blood glucose levels.

Humans require a stable internal environment to function effectively. The maintenance of this internal environment within tolerable limits is called homeostasis. Humans survive in their natural external environment based on the physiology of their internal environment. Homeostasis is a dynamic process, with continual monitoring of the body's biochemical and physical status. The nervous and endocrine body organ systems provide control and regulation of the body's internal biochemical and physical environments.

All living organisms have a boundary that separates their internal environment from the external environment. In single cell organisms it is the cell membrane that acts as this boundary. In complex multicellular organisms an external boundary is formed by the integumentary system. This system protects internal organs from drying out and forms a boundary layer between the internal and external environments. This is one of the functions of our skin. At a cellular level a semi-permeable membrane surrounds all cells to maintain the internal environment of each cell.

Homeostasis is one of the fundamental characteristics of living things and the normal functioning of the body requires biochemical and physical parameters to be maintained around a set point, just like a temperature setting on a central heating thermostat. When the desired temperature is achieved, the heating system is switched off and when the temperature drops below the desired setting, the heating system is switched on.

Homeostatic control mechanisms act to reduce the change in the internal environment to achieve the body's set point for each biochemical and physical parameter. These parameters include body temperature, blood pH, blood glucose level and electrolyte balance. Figure 5 indicates that small fluctuations occur around the average state for each parameter. Homeostatic control is achieved by the process of negative *feedback*. The process of negative feedback control is illustrated in Figure 6.

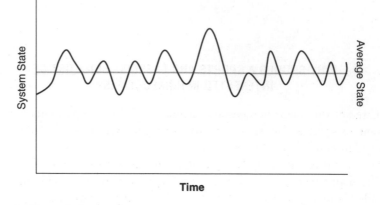

Figure 5   *Homeostasis*

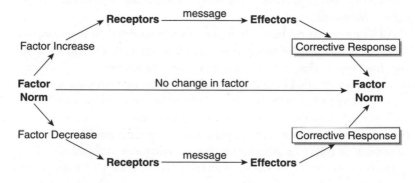

Figure 6   *Negative feedback control*

Exercise disrupts homeostasis through the demands placed on the body, the metabolic consequences of increased energy expenditure and subsequent changes in the biochemical and physical conditions in the body. Nutrition also influences homeostasis of blood glucose, water and electrolyte conditions in the body. External conditions can also play a part in disturbing the homeostatic balance of thermoregulation and this is where we will start to conceptualise homeostasis in the world of sport and exercise.

THERMOREGULATION – HOMEOSTASIS OF BODY TEMPERATURE

In humans the core temperature is maintained at 37°C while the shell temperature can vary between less than 20°C and 40°C, depending on the external environment. The core temperature and highest temperature in the body is found in the skull and thoracic and abdominal cavities where body organs are located. At the heat-loss surface area, which is the skin, the shell temperature is lower and the skin is less vulnerable to temperature changes.

WHY IS THERMOREGULATION IMPORTANT IN THE HUMAN BODY?

Temperature extremes cause tissue damage. High temperatures cause the proteins in our cells to denature, which means that they unfold from their complex structure. Proteins do not function properly when they are unfolded and this will affect enzymes, cell organelles and cells. When cells are frozen, damage results because water turns to ice crystals. This can lead to frostbite, a serious condition that requires medical attention. Cooling causes vasoconstriction in blood vessels in the skin and this leads to reduced blood flow and a decrease in oxygen supply to cells.

Temperature also influences the rate of chemical reactions in the body. At low temperatures the rate of reactions is slowed and normal functioning is reduced. Cold-water hypothermia can quickly reduce the core temperature to such an extent that respiratory and circulatory failure can result. This is due to the impact of temperature reduction on electrical activity in the brain and heart.

HOW DOES THE BODY MAINTAIN ITS NORMAL TEMPERATURE?

The regulation of body temperature is dependent upon the balance between heat production and heat loss. The metabolic functions of all cells produce heat in proportion to their metabolic activity. The hypothalamus is the thermoregulatory centre of the body, containing central thermoreceptors that directly monitor the core temperature of blood flowing through the brain.

Peripheral thermoreceptors in the skin respond to the temperature of the external environment and send this information to the hypothalamus.

The hypothalamus then sends nerve pulses to effector tissues/organs for temperature regulation mechanisms to be switched on. Blood plays a crucial role in transferring heat from the core to the shell of the body. This increases the thermal gradient between the body and the external environment which speeds up heat loss. This can work against the body when the external temperature is much lower than that of the body, for example, when falling into cold water.

Mechanisms of body temperature regulation

Once the hypothalamus has detected a move away from the temperature set point, the body responds to bring the body temperature back to the set point. This is a classic negative feedback control mechanism. The hypothalamus sends signals to four effectors to restore normal temperature.

When the core temperature rises, arteriole blood vessels in the skin dilate when the hypothalamus signals to smooth muscle in the arteriole walls to relax. Blood flow to the skin is increased and this allows more heat to be transferred from the core to the shell. When core body temperature decreases, the hypothalamus sends signals to the arteriole blood vessels to constrict and reduce the flow of blood to the periphery of the body. This reduces the heat transfer from the core to the shell. Vasodilation increases blood flow to the skin resulting in a larger surface area through which heat is lost to the external environment. Vasoconstriction occurs when temperature in the body drops and blood vessels become constricted so that minimal heat loss occurs.

Sweat glands are stimulated to produce sweat; as the sweat evaporates it removes heat from the body. Increased sweating contributes to heat loss through the energy dissipated when water vaporises, taking away heat so that body temperature is reduced. Evaporation of sweat from the skin reduces heat by 0.58 kcal.ml^{-1} of sweat. The consequence of this mechanism of heat loss is water and electrolyte loss in the sweat. In endurance events such as running a marathon, an athlete can lose between 0.8L.hr^{-1} and 1.2L.hr^{-1} for cool to warm and warm to hot weather respectively.

In cold conditions skeletal muscle can generate heat through the process of shivering. This occurs when the hypothalamus sends signals to the motor control area of the brain that then stimulates a cycle of involuntary contraction and relaxation.

Endocrine glands respond to the body cooling and act to increase metabolic rate and heat production. The thyroid gland releases thyroxine, a hormone that increases metabolic rate in cells, which speeds up the rate of chemical reactions that produce heat. The adrenal glands respond by producing more adrenalin and noradrenalin, these hormones also speeding up the metabolic rate of cells.

OSMOREGULATION – THE CONTROL OF BODY WATER

Water is a remarkable nutrient and one that needs daily replenishment for optimal body function. A human's body mass is made up of 40 to 70 per cent of water, depending on age, gender, body composition and acute physiological state. Water is found throughout the body, defined in two fluid compartments. Extracellular fluid refers to the fluid between (outside) cells and includes blood plasma and intercellular fluid, the fluid inside cells. Water moves through the process of osmosis. Euhydration is the term for the normal set point for water concentration in the body and this is achieved by maintaining the water concentration gradient between cells and blood plasma. Osmoregulation is the regulation of water concentration in blood plasma: it controls the amount of water available for cells to absorb.

The homeostatic control of water in the body occurs through a negative feedback control system. This system includes the hypothalamus and pituitary glands and the water excretion organs, the kidneys. Osmoreceptors are located in the hypothalamus, these receptors being capable of detecting water concentration in blood plasma. Figure 7 indicates how this negative feedback mechanism works. When the water concentration decreases, the hypothalamus sends chemical messages to the pituitary gland to produce anti-diuretic hormone (ADH), which acts on the kidneys to maintain water levels. ADH alters the tubules of the kidney to become more or less permeable to water. During dehydration more ADH is released and this stimulates the kidneys to reabsorb more water. It does this by making kidney tubules more permeable to water. In this case urine becomes more concentrated and takes on a yellow colour. Urine colour is widely used as a simple measure of hydration status. When there is too much water in the blood, this is detected by the hypothalamus and it signals the pituitary to secrete less ADH. When we drink more water than is required, the body maintains its optimal water content by excreting water.

Be aware that this simple explanation for water is complicated by the ionic concentrations for sodium and potassium.

Even mild dehydration reduces blood volume, which reduces blood flow to the muscles, organs and glands, along with oxygen and nutrients

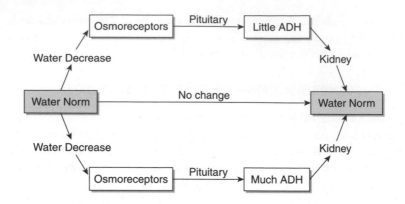

Figure 7   *Osmoregulation*

since these are also carried in the blood. The ability to expel heat is also lost since skin circulation is reduced, elevating the core temperature of the body. Research undertaken in a range of sport and physical activity contexts suggests that dehydration occurs even in winter conditions when it is cold and wet. Also, by the time you feel thirsty you are already dehydrated, which is why education on appropriate hydration strategies is important for both sports performers and recreational walkers out for a day's walk. In sports performance it is not unusual for competitors to lose up to a litre of fluid per hour. Levels of dehydration experienced without appropriate drinking strategies will cause difficulties in both physical and mental performance, affecting speed of movement and distance covered in team games as well as decision making.

BLOOD GLUCOSE HOMEOSTASIS

Two hormones are principally responsible for controlling the concentration of glucose in the blood. These are insulin and glucagon. Figure 8 illustrates the principle of negative feedback control for blood sugar levels.

Receptors in the pancreas monitor blood glucose levels and stimulate two different types of hormone-releasing cells, insulin-releasing cells and glucagon-releasing cells. Blood glucose levels are affected by nutrient intake and exercise. When glucose levels increase, e.g. after a sugar-rich meal, insulin is released by the pancreas and targets the liver. Glucose is converted to glycogen and stored in the liver. When glucose

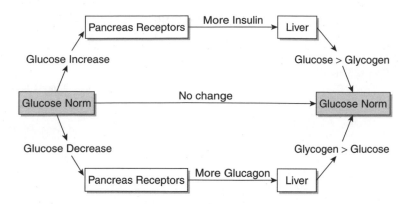

Figure 8   *Blood glucose homeostasis*

levels decrease, in the case of acute exercise, more glucagon is released by the pancreas and this stimulates the liver to convert glycogen to glucose. Glucose is made available in the blood and maintains a fuel source for cells.

Many sports drinks contain carbohydrate in the form of glucose, with rehydration drinks containing smaller percentages of glucose compared to energy drinks. Sports drinks high in glucose concentration taken half an hour before exercise can negatively effect your blood glucose just at the time you are starting to exercise. Understanding homeostatic control of blood glucose is therefore important for sport and exercise scientists who advise coaches and athletes on use of sports drinks.

Regular acute disturbances of homeostasis lead to chronic adaptations in the body's responses to exercise. Highly trained athletes become more tolerant to biochemical and physical changes in the body. Understanding homeostasis is important for sports and exercise scientists so that they can assist in the design of appropriate training programmes, coupled with diet and fluid requirements before, during and after exercise in training, competition or physical activity. Changes in environmental conditions, such as temperature and humidity, the physical demands of an exercise challenge, the pace or effort selected by the participant, the clothing worn, the food and fluid consumed before, during and after sport or physical activity will all influence homeostatic control mechanisms in the body either positively or negatively.

FURTHER READING

Marieb, E.N. (2003) *Anatomy and Physiology*. San Francisco: Pearson Education.
Tortora, G.J. (2005) *Principles of Anatomy and Physiology*, 11th edn. Chichester John Wiley & Sons.

MIKE GRAY
CARLTON COOKE

Muscles, Strength and Power

The relative importance of strength and power varies widely in different sports. In particular, in sports such as weightlifting, throwing, jumping and sprinting events, strength and power are very important for maximisation of performance, while for other sports such as marathon running and pistol shooting, they are much less important.

A plethora of factors can affect the ability of the human body to generate force or torque (turning force): the type of muscular actions (eccentric, concentric, isometric, isokinetic), the length of the muscles, the speed of movement, the cross-sectional and physiological cross-sectional area of the muscles, the number and type of muscle fibres stimulated, the frequency of stimulation, the joint angle, lever length and body size.

The scope of this chapter is to explain how muscle growth can affect the ability of humans to generate force and torque and potentially improve sports performance.

Strength is generally known as the ability to exert force or torque. It has been defined as the peak force or torque developed during a maximal voluntary contraction under a given set of conditions. Force is the product of the mass of an object and its linear acceleration (force = mass × acceleration, SI unit: Newton or N) and torque is a measure of the turning effects of a force on a lever [torque (τ) = force (F) × lever arm distance (r) or moment arm, SI unit: Newton-metre or Nm].

Power is the product of strength and speed. Power can be defined as the rate at which mechanical work (W) is performed per unit time (T), (i.e. P = W/T), or as the product of force (F) and velocity (V) (P = F×V).

Skeletal muscles constitute approximately 50 per cent of the fat-free mass (all tissues excluding fat) of human bodies and their main function is force generation. Skeletal muscle (e.g. quadriceps) is comprised of muscle fibres (muscle cells), which are made up of myofibrils (each muscle fibre consists of myofibrils that tend to extend the whole length of the muscle fibre), and these myofibrils are made up of sarcomeres (the contractile elements of muscle fibres that are composed of thin and thick filaments of actin and myosin respectively).

The maintenance and growth of skeletal muscle is a very complex process that can be affected by many factors including strength training, genetics, nutrition, endocrine system function and disease. The genotype (genetic characteristics of a person) is accountable for the phenotype or the observable characteristics. However, environmental factors such as training can also influence the phenotype of an individual. The capacity of skeletal muscle for adaptive change (myoplasticity) governs to a great extent the degree of improvement in strength and/or power, as the muscle adapts with either treatment or training. In other words, the magnitude of change and improvement in either strength or power lies within the muscle.

Muscle growth has been primarily thought to be the result of hypertrophy or increase in muscle size by addition of myofibrils. The cross-sectional area (diameter) of a muscle fibre increases mainly as additional myofilaments of myosin and actin are added to each myofibril leading to splitting and increased number of myofibrils. Muscle growth as a result of hyperplasia would require the addition of new muscle fibres. There is little evidence in humans to suggest that hyperplasia of skeletal muscle occurs in adult humans; to our knowledge there is only one longitudinal study (12 weeks of resistance training, 3 times per week) that has provided some evidence of hyperplasia in healthy human subjects. However, hyperplasia does take place during the prenatal and postnatal period, with humans reaching their full number of muscle cells soon after they are born.

Strength training or progressive resistance exercise is considered one of the most effective ways to enhance muscle growth. It is well established that strength training can induce muscle hypertrophy that can become evident after six to seven weeks of resistance training. However, hypertrophy through training can only be achieved in the presence of a diet that supplies adequate nutrients to meet energy demands as well as the necessary materials to build new muscle.

Muscles with a large cross-sectional area tend to produce more force than muscles with smaller ones; the main reason being that bigger

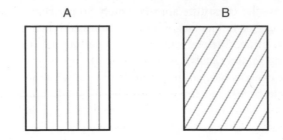

Figure 9 *A (parallel muscle), B (pennate muscle)*

muscles have a greater number of sarcomeres, thus greater potential for generating force.

The physiological cross-sectional area is somewhat different from the cross-sectional area of a particular muscle; this is because the arrangement of fascicles (bundles of skeletal muscle fibres) within the muscles may form different patterns in regard to the tendons (Figure 9).

Pennate muscles, for example, are flat muscles with their fibres arranged around one or more central tendons like the barbs of a feather. The angle of pennation can affect the number of sarcomeres within the muscle and consequently force production. Pennation allows the packing of more muscle fibres per cross-sectional area thus generating greater force. Independently of angle of pennation, increase in muscle size usually leads to increase in strength.

The cross-sectional area of two different muscles appears to be the same. However, the physiological cross-sectional area of muscle B is greater than muscle A because of the higher number of fibres within the muscle (Figure 9).

KEY POINTS

- Hypertrophy (and not hyperplasia), mainly as a result of resistance training, can be accomplished only in the presence of a diet that provides all the nutrients needed to build new muscle.
- Hypertrophy in turn might result in an improvement in strength and power, thus leading to enhanced performance in sports where strength and power are of primary importance.
- Muscle growth is only one of the factors that can potentially improve strength, power and ultimately sports performance through progressive resistance training.

FURTHER READING

Baechle, T.R. and Earle, R.W. (eds) (2000) *Essentials of Strength Training and Conditioning*. Champaign, IL: Human Kinetics.

Komi, P.V. (2003) *Strength and Power in Sport*, 2nd edn. Oxford: Blackwell Science.

Kraemer, W.J. and Hakkinen, K. (2002) *Strength Training for Sport*. Oxford: Blackwell.

THEOCHARIS ISPOGLOU

·Energy Systems

The human body needs a supply of energy for all its functions, including exercise, which is sourced through the foods we consume daily as dietary carbohydrate, fat and protein. These can be used as fuels in the form of glucose, free fatty acids and amino acids.

The energy currency in most processes in the body is adenosine triphosphate (ATP). Energy is released from ATP when one of the phosphate groups is removed through the process of hydrolysis (a chemical process in which a substance is split into simpler compounds by the addition of water) releasing 7.3 kcal of energy per mole of ATP. Metabolic pathways exist within the body that both exploit the energy of ATP but also ensure the resynthesis of ATP from available fuels. Metabolism is the total of all energy transformations that occur within the body.

Energy systems exist as catabolic pathways that ensure that the synthesis of ATP meets demand. These metabolic pathways involve processing of fuels through distinct sets of enzyme reactions ultimately leading to energy transfer. The store of ATP in all cells is limited but its synthesis is matched by rephosphorylation of ADP on demand. In muscles these systems combine anaerobic and aerobic components to provide ATP synthesis and ensure the constant availability of energy to power muscle contractions by using energy released from the breakdown of ATP.

The ATP-CP system is the simplest of the three energy systems and does not require oxygen (anaerobic). The store of ATP in the muscles is limited

energy systems

51

and is only sufficient to generate energy for several seconds during maximal exercise. To enable maximal exercise to continue, ATP must be resynthesised, whereby ADP is rephosphylated to ATP by CP, a reaction which is catalysed by the enzyme creatine kinase. However, the CP stores will only support maximal exercise for approximately ten seconds. Beyond this point the body must rely on other energy systems to provide ATP.

In all cells as well as muscle, the glycolytic system is the metabolic pathway responsible for the initial metabolism of glucose under both aerobic and anaerobic conditions. The fuels for this system may be derived from all dietary sources of carbohydrate but ultimately, these are processed into glucose or its intermediates for metabolism.

Glycolysis is a set of 11 enzyme-catalysed reactions located within the cytoplasm of the muscle fibre. These reactions begin with glucose or glycogen (the stored form of glucose found in the muscle and liver) and end with the production of pyruvate. Under aerobic conditions pyruvate can be oxidised and enters the tricarboxylic acid cycle (Krebs Cycle), whereas under anaerobic conditions pyruvate is converted to lactate. Glycolysis is essential whether metabolism is anaerobic or aerobic.

The yield of ATP purely from glycolysis is small (2 ATP). The process can be very fast so that high rates of supply can be sustained, but only for short periods of time. Excess lactate accumulation under anaerobic conditions will impair enzyme function, including glycolysis.

Oxidative metabolism occurs in the mitochondria where fuels like pyruvate (from glycolysis) or free fatty acids (from dietary fat or adipose tissue) are oxidised fully with a high yield of ATP. The oxidative system is the primary fuel source for endurance events lasting longer than two minutes.

In the presence of oxygen, pyruvate is converted to acetyl Coenzyme A (acetyl Co A), which enters Krebs Cycle. There is complete oxidation of fuels into carbon dioxide and water alongside electron transfer into the electron transport chain, resulting in ATP synthesis. The oxidation of fuels into carbon dioxide and the reduction of oxygen to water are tightly coupled; the whole process is called oxidative phosphorylation. A proton gradient is generated to drive the rephosphorylation of ADP, with a total energy yield of 38 ATP per mole of glucose.

The stores of glycogen within the body are limited, lasting between 90–120 minutes in hard exercise; however, the stores of fat are very large and can maintain low intensity aerobic exercise for much longer periods of time, lasting days. The form of fat that is metabolised to produce ATP is free fatty acids (FFAs). Once these enter the muscle fibre, they are enzymatically activated with ATP and prepared for oxidation within the mitochondria. This process of β oxidation converts the FFAs to acetyl Co A, which then follows the same path via the Krebs Cycle and electron transport chain as glucose. However, the yield of ATP is considerably greater, at 129 moles.

Fat is metabolised at a much slower rate than carbohydrate, which means that it is rate-limited and unable to support the provision of ATP in high-intensity exercise, but can support low-intensity exercise for long periods of time.

The third fuel is protein, which may be used oxidatively in extreme circumstances (e.g. starvation or acute glycogen depletion) through the catabolism of amino acids. However, depending on the circumstances, negative energy balance may ensue.

In summary, each energy system operates simultaneously. The relative contribution of each will vary depending upon intensity and duration of exercise, as well as upon the availability of oxygen and fuels.

KEY POINTS

- ATP is the energy currency within the body and releases 7.3 kcal of energy per mole of ATP, but is a renewable energy source. The quantity of ATP at any instance would last one to two seconds unless replaced.
- Glycolysis is the primary system to initiate metabolism of glucose, which it can perform without oxygen (anaerobic). Though fast at producing energy, it is inefficient, only yielding 2 ATP per mole of glucose, along with the associated biochemical intermediary of lactic acid.
- The aerobic energy system for the complete oxidation of fuels operates with high efficiency, but only in the presence of oxygen (aerobic). Oxidative metabolism of fat may be efficient but it is not as rapid as the metabolism of carbohydrate and is rate-limited, which means that, continued exercise is only possible at a slower pace.

FURTHER READING

McArdle, W.D., Katch, F.I. and Katch, V.L. (2006) *Exercise Physiology: Energy, Nutrition, and Human Performance*, 6th edn. Philadelphia, PA: Lippincott, Williams & Wilkins.
Wilmore, J.H. and Costill, D.L. (2004) *Physiology for Sport and Exercise*, 3rd edn. Champaign, IL: Human Kinetics.

JOHN O'HARA

Energy Balance and Body Composition

Energy balance represents the difference between energy intake and energy expenditure and is fundamental to health and physical performance.

$$\text{Energy balance (EB)} = \text{Energy intake (EI)} - \text{Energy expenditure (EE)}$$

If EI > EE, then EB is *positive* and energy is *stored* in the body. If EI < EE, then EB is *negative* and energy is *lost* from the body.

Changes in energy balance and energy stores over a period of a few days are reflected by changes in body mass, as defined by the First Law of Thermodynamics. The energy (fuel) stores of the body comprise glycogen, fat and protein. Glycogen is the body's store of carbohydrate and is contained mainly within skeletal muscles ($\approx$ 80%) and the liver ($\approx$ 20%). Protein stores (in skeletal, cardiac and smooth muscle) are not a preferred form of energy and are normally only used as a 'last resort'; e.g. during starvation and endurance exercise (> two hours) when glycogen stores are inadequate.

ENERGY INTAKE

Energy intake is derived from the diet and is determined by the amounts and types of foods eaten. Energy intake is commonly expressed in kilocalories (kcal) or kilojoules (kJ), usually over 24 hours as kcal/day or kJ/day. Note that 1 kcal = 4.183 kJ. Nutrients within foods that provide energy are called macronutrients and comprise carbohydrates, fats and proteins. The energy values of these macronutrients per unit mass are approximately as follows:

Carbohydrate – 16 kJ/g
Fat – 39 kJ/g
Protein – 17 kJ/g

Energy intake may be assessed by recording all food and beverage intake in a diary over a given period of time. Foods may be recorded as portion sizes, or preferably as weighed amounts. The data from the food diary may then be analysed either manually, which entails looking up each food in a table of food composition, recording its nutrients for a given quantity, and adding them up in tables, or by entering specific quantities of each food consumed into a computer database of the nutrient content of common foods. Modern software programmes calculate energy values and nutrient quantities for specified amounts of different foods listed in the database. Also, these programmes often compare energy and nutrient intakes of an individual to the standard Recommended Nutrient Intake (RNI) for the individual's age, sex, body mass and activity level. Measuring energy intake and macronutrient contributions is used to assess the input side of the energy balance equation. It is important for both the athlete who is training hard and needs enough energy to sustain a very active lifestyle and a less active person who wishes to maintain their weight, body composition and macronutrient contributions to optimise their health status.

ENERGY EXPENDITURE

In adults, energy expenditure reflects basal metabolism, the thermic effect of food (i.e. digestion, absorption and assimilation), thermoregulation (maintenance of a constant deep body temperature) and physical activity. In children, energy is required for the same functions as in adults; however, an extra amount beyond that in adults is required to support growth and maturation. Children need to be in positive energy balance to enable a net synthesis and deposition of tissues. Energy expenditure per unit body mass is therefore higher in children than in adults.

A number of techniques may be employed to measure energy expenditure, and these vary in terms of their accuracy, reliability and expense. Perhaps the most accurate and direct technique involves a human calorimeter, which measures the body's heat production over a specified period of time. Human calorimetry is based upon the knowledge that essentially all food metabolised in respiration is ultimately converted to heat energy, as defined by the Second Law of Thermodynamics. However, whole-body human calorimeters are not widely available, are expensive to construct and operate, and they do not permit the evaluation of 'free living' energy expenditure.

Energy expenditure can also be measured indirectly and cheaply, by collecting an individual's expired air over a known period of time and calculating oxygen consumption (in L/min) using the Haldane equation. Oxygen consumption is proportional to energy expenditure if an individual is in a physiological 'steady state', which occurs when the oxygen demand of the whole body is equal to oxygen supply over a period of a few minutes. The body is normally in steady state at rest and during light exercise. An example of a non-steady state situation is that occurring during anaerobic exercise, for which a proportion of energy is generated by the active muscles without oxygen. Measurements of oxygen consumption therefore underestimate energy expenditure when the body is not in a steady state or rate of aerobic energy expenditure.

Measuring energy expenditure through calculating oxygen consumption from expired air analysis is a cornerstone of fitness testing used by exercise physiologists when assessing high-performance athletes recreationally active individuals or cardiac patients in a hospital environment. Maximal oxygen consumption, which is the maximum amount of oxygen you can take in, transport and utilise in exercising muscles is a measure of aerobic potential in high-performance endurance athletes and in others reflects in part their training status. Oxygen consumption can also tell us how economical individuals are in performing various activities, which can also predict their performance in events such as long-distance running.

Another technique, which is considered to be accurate, reliable and allows individuals to adhere to their habitual lifestyles, is the doubly labelled water method. This is a non-invasive technique that involves the administration of two stable isotopes of water ($^{2}H_2O$ and $H_2^{18}O$) followed by serial urine collections over a period of $\approx$ two weeks. The method is based upon the principle that $^{2}H_2O$ is lost from the body in water alone, whereas $H_2^{18}O$ is lost both in water and as CO_2. The rate of CO_2 production can thus be calculated from the difference in the rates of turnover of these two isotopes. With a knowledge of dietary composition and hence, the fuel mixture oxidised, energy expenditure may be estimated.

Basal metabolic rate (BMR) is the rate of energy expenditure necessary to sustain basal bodily functions and is the minimum energy requirement of survival. Resting metabolic rate (RMR) is equal to BMR plus the thermic effect of food and thermoregulation. Various equations for estimating BMR and RMR have been produced from actual measurements of BMR made in populations. These include the Schofield equation and the Harris–Benedict equation.

ENERGY EXPENDITURE OF PHYSICAL ACTIVITY

Physical activity may have a profound effect on the rate of energy expenditure, and exercise that involves the recruitment of a large muscle mass greatly elevates energy expenditure above RMR. For example, in adults, during sustained, whole-body aerobic activity (> 5 min), metabolic rate may increase 10 to 20-fold above RMR, whereas during short-lived (< 1 min) maximal intensity anaerobic activity, a momentary 40- to 50-fold elevation of RMR is possible. The energy expenditure of physical activity may be expressed as multiples of RMR, described as 'metabolic equivalent' (MET) values, where 1 MET equates to resting metabolic rate (RMR). An activity that raises RMR 10-fold, is therefore designated a MET value of 10. The energy expenditure of physical activity can be obtained through records (a diary) of physical activity. An example of the calculation of the energy expenditure of a bout of exercise is as follows for an individual with an RMR of 1663 k cal/day:

$$1 \text{ day } (24 \text{ hr} \times 60 \text{ min}) = 1440 \text{ minutes}$$

Therefore, RMR per minute equates to $1663/1440 = 1.16$ k cal/min.

If the individual runs for 30 minutes at an energy expenditure of 12.4 METS then the energy 'cost' of their run is $30 \times 12.4 \times 1.16 = 432$ k cal.

The MET values of different activities are listed in various books, including the recommended text at the end of this chapter. When collecting physical activity data from an individual, it is practical to divide the 24 hours in a day into 15-minute slots. The duration, to the nearest 15 minutes, of all activities can then be noted in a 24-hour diary. Sometimes it is convenient to compile activities into a single category and designate each category a MET value. For example:

1 MET = sleeping, lying relaxed, watching television;
3–4 METS = leisurely walking, swimming or cycling; various indoor play activities (children); housework;
5–8 METS = outdoor play, including ball games; fast walking, jogging, swimming, cycling (not racing);
9–12 METS = vigorous sports, running, squash, competitive tennis;
>12 METS = high-performance sports including middle-distance running, race cycling/swimming.

BODY COMPOSITION

Body composition describes the structural components of the body, which include energy stores that may be readily mobilised for the production of ATP (the energy currency in the body used by muscles to power contractions). The structural components may be divided into lean and fat mass. Fat is stored as triglyceride in adipose tissue, both under the skin and internally around the major organs and is by far the largest energy store, even within lean athletes. Lean mass is the amount of body mass that is not fat (i.e. body mass – fat mass) and comprises mainly water, together with structural protein, connective tissue and minerals.

Understanding body composition and how to measure it are important for sport and exercise scientists for a number of reasons. For example, obesity is assessed based on body composition, but many forms of measurement do not assess fat mass or proportion directly. The most commonly quoted assessment of obesity is body mass index (BMI = weight (kg)/height^2(m)), which does not discriminate between the different components of fat and lean tissue. While BMI is acceptable for categorising groups of people, it does not work well for certain individuals, particularly athletes who have a high muscle mass. Some of the fittest, most powerful and lean athletes are therefore incorrectly categorised as obese by BMI because it uses weight and muscle is denser than fat. Understanding these differences is important for supporting and advising those who are overweight and who start to regularly exercise as they will often not lose weight or even put it on as they lose less dense fat but gain in more dense muscle mass. This is one example of where integrating an understanding of body composition with energy balance is important.

Body composition is difficult to measure accurately in humans because there is no technique that quantifies all the components directly. Despite the existence of a variety of techniques, all depend upon making various assumptions, which are built into mathematical equations. To assess body composition, the body is considered to comprise two or more components: fat and lean mass, with lean mass often being subdivided into water, muscle and bone. These components of lean mass can be assessed individually via different methods.

One of the most accurate and reliable methods for assessing body composition at present is dual energy x-ray absorptiometry (DXA). DXA quantifies bone mineral and estimates fat and muscle mass for the body as a whole, or in its different regions. Other methods include underwater weighing and air displacement plethysmography, which measure body volume, from which body density can be calculated if body mass is known. Bioelectric impedance analysis estimates total body water. The technique is based upon the concept that water is a high conductor of electricity. A low-level current is passed across the body and the resistance to flow (impedance) is measured. Since fat is virtually anhydrous, there is a relationship between electrical impedance and relative body fat content.

A cheap and accessible way to assess body fat content and the distribution of subcutaneous fat is to use skinfold calipers to measure the thickness of skinfolds at specified sites in the body. The technique involves pinching the skin between the pincers of the calipers which record the thickness of the double layer of skin, fat and water. Experience and practice are required to produce accurate readings. The readings may be entered into a series of mathematical equations to estimate the percentage of body mass that comprises fat. Different equations are used for men and women and for athletes and non-athletes because of the effects of sex and training on the distribution of internal and subcutaneous fat.

FURTHER READING

McArdle, W.D., Katch, F.I. and Katch, V.L. (2006) *Exercise Physiology, Energy, Nutrition, and Human Performance*, 6th edn. Philadelphia, PA: Lippincott, Williams & Wilkins.
Whitney, E.N. and Rolfes, S.R (2005) *Understanding Nutrition*. London: Thomson and Wadsworth.

CATHY ZANKER
LOUISE SUTTON

Principles of Training

The aim of training is to maintain or improve performance or health. In terms of exercise physiology, training is about stimulating structural and functional adaptations in the body to be able to perform better in selected tasks within sport or to maintain or improve health status. In order to stimulate the body to produce the required adaptations, a training programme is required that incorporates repeated bouts of planned exercise to stimulate acute responses in the body. If the training programme is appropriately planned and adhered to, it will result in chronic adaptations over time which will result in improved performance, be it in strength, speed, power endurance or other components of fitness, with the combination of adaptations dependent on the focus of the training programme. Effective training programmes are based on the application of training principles, the primary principles being progressive overload, specificity, individuality and reversibility.

Progressive overload is a combination of two principles of training, overload and progression. The application of the principle of overload in training is what stimulates an improvement in physiological function to produce a training response, which results in improved performance in one or more of the components of fitness (e.g. strength). Overload in training is achieved by manipulating the intensity, frequency and duration, most often with a focus on a particular type or mode of exercise, although for multi-eventers such as triathletes or decathletes this is not so straightforward. FITT is often used to summarise the principle of overload (FITT = Frequency, Intensity, Time and Type).

Manipulation of progression in the application of overload is a critical component of planning and delivering effective training programmes. The cycle of overload needs to be carefully manipulated through periodic training. Overload beyond the current capacity of the individual will stimulate complex and integrated functional adaptations from the molecular to the system level of the body, which, linked with appropriate periods of recovery, will result in an enhancement or super-compensation in performance. If progression is attempted through changes which are too large and the training repeatedly and doggedly adhered to by the individual, the result will be a decrease in performance rather than an increase, with an increased probability of injury, staleness, over-reaching and over-training. This is why careful planning, monitoring and evaluation are required to ensure effective training adaptations.

The specificity principle relates to adaptations to training that are very specific. The specificity of training applies to the mode or type of exercise, the muscles, the speed of movement, the range of motion, the intensity of the exercise, the energy systems engaged, etc. Specificity therefore tells us that only the performance of the particular movements used in the chosen sport or exercise can be 100 per cent applicable to training. Therefore it is important to consider the extent of carry-over or transfer from training to the sport. For example, in strength training it is important to select appropriate exercises to target the particular muscle groups involved in the particular movement pattern in the sport. However, it is also important to consider the timing, recruitment and intensity of muscle contributions and try to mimic as closely as possible the specific movement patterns from the sport to maximise the transfer or carry-over.

If two athletes subject themselves to exactly the same training programme they will respond to it differently, which exemplifies the principle of individuality in training. A number of factors influence the individual nature of training response. These include training history and state of fitness at the start of a training programme, genetic blueprint or predisposition and other factors like age and gender. Genetics defines the potential each of us has for development in the various components of fitness, as well as the rate at which we will approach that potential. It is true that Olympic and world champions have chosen the right parents (i.e. they have a more optimum predisposition or blueprint) but, without exposure to appropriate training programmes, they will not be able to reach their potential. Individuality therefore explains why we have to plan, monitor and evaluate training on an individual basis, as copying better performers' training programmes may result in over-training or injury.

Related to individuality is the law or principle of diminishing returns. This principle relates to our understanding that sedentary individuals beginning a training programme will experience much greater improvements in a given time than high-performance athletes who have been training hard for many years. As number of years of training increase the percentage improvement in performance over a given time diminishes, as we approach our genetic potential. High-performance athletes therefore do not expect to make significant improvements in their performance, but accept that they have to work very hard for protracted periods of time to see only very small improvements. Such improvements can, however, make the difference between winning a medal and not making a final at major championships, as the magnitude of difference in performance at the top of most sports is now very small.

If you stop training or reduce your training load considerably your fitness and level of performance will decrease. In the same way that the molecules, tissues, organs and systems of the human body adapt to the stimulus of training so increasing fitness, they will also adapt to the stimulus of detraining by reverting back to their pre-training status. The effects of detraining have been shown to be significant after a couple of weeks of inactivity, which is commonly associated with injury in sport. For example, after two weeks of inactivity decreases of about 3 and 5 per cent have been shown in muscle strength and cardiorespiratory fitness. Interestingly, anaerobic performance seems to decline at a slower rate than strength and cardiorespiratory fitness. The rate and magnitude of the effects of detraining will vary between individuals and will also depend on the length of time of detraining, the training history and the performance levels prior to detraining. Reversibility and detraining should not be confused with tapering, which is where athletes cut down their training in preparation for a major championship or trial. Tapering allows performers to be at their best as they will have decreased their training load so that they are fresh and hungry for competition, but this is done in a controlled way as part of their planned training programme. In certain circumstances, where peak performance is not required, athletes will train through championships, working towards the main goals of their training programme, which are set so that they can peak for the major championship of the competitive season or year.

Applying the principles of training to planning, monitoring and evaluating training programmes is important for athletes and coaches, so that realistic goals can be set and the best opportunity to achieve the desired performance improvements can be realised.

FURTHER READING

Baechle, T.R. and Earle, R.W. (eds) (2000) *Essentials of Strength Training and Conditioning*. Champaign, IL: Human Kinetics.
Kraemer, W.J. and Hakkinen, K. (2002) *Strength Training for Sport*. Oxford: Blackwell.

CARLTON COOKE

Fitness for Sport and Health

FITNESS FOR SPORT

Fitness may be described as the possession of a characteristic or a series of characteristics that allow the performance of a given task. Thus fitness for sport may be seen as being specific in nature. To illustrate the point, one only has to compare the physical make-up of an elite-level basketball player with that of a marathon runner. The former will generally be tall and quite well muscled, particularly in the upper body. They will need to be very fast and agile, with the ability to jump high and to perform repeated bouts of high-intensity work with relatively short periods of recovery. The marathon runner is likely to be relatively slight and very lean. Their activity requires them to run at a sub-maximal, but fast pace continuously for more than two hours. The two activities are very different in duration and intensity and require different physical attributes and draw on the three **Energy Systems** in differing ratios. In sport, therefore, people tend to gravitate towards activities for which they have the appropriate characteristics or attributes. Thus fitness in sport may be referred to as 'sport- or performance-specific fitness'.

FITNESS FOR HEALTH

It is not only sport that requires us to be fit. We also need to be fit for everyday life. We need to have the capability to perform the tasks of daily life. From time to time we are called upon to be physically strong, when lifting heavy weights such as a parcel, some furniture, or to support someone who is unsteady on their feet or who has fallen. We may need to stretch to reach something on a high shelf, to be fast and powerful to run quickly up a flight of stairs or have the muscular endurance to mop a large area of flooring or to trim a large hedgerow. There is also a wealth of research evidence supporting a positive association and relationship between health status and physical activity and fitness, in terms of disease prevention. It is well established that being fit and active reduces the incidence of certain diseases. These diseases include: coronary heart disease, type 2 diabetes mellitus, most forms of cancer and diseases of the blood such as hyperlipidemia and hypercholsterolaemia. This type of fitness is sometimes referred to as health-related fitness.

Components of fitness for sport and health

- *Whole-body aerobic endurance*. This is sometimes referred to as cardiovascular endurance, cardiorespiratory endurance or stamina, the latter being the common lay term. This aspect of fitness requires a powerful heart able to pump relatively large volumes of blood with each beat, lungs free from disease and airways that are clear and large muscle masses necessary to exercise. Sports performers with high levels of aerobic capability are typically involved in middle- and long-distance running or cycling, long-distance swimming and in games will tend to play in the 'link' or midfield positions. In health-related fitness, good aerobic fitness usually means having a healthy heart, good circulation and healthy lungs.

- *Local muscular endurance*. This means being able to repeat a muscular movement for a certain amount of time. Rowing will involve many repetitions of the pulling action and is likely to be continuous. It will require good muscular endurance in many different muscle groups of the upper body, legs and trunk. Tennis may involve lots of swings of the racquet, but with rest intervals of differing durations. In everyday life, sawing or chopping wood requires muscle endurance of the arms, hands and shoulders.

- *Muscular strength and power*. In sport this can be sustained strength such as in a tug of war where a tug may be an all-out effort for up to 60 seconds or so. In rock climbing, it may mean having to raise the whole body when only being able to grip with two fingers and a thumb. In daily life this may mean moving large pieces of furniture, or helping an infirm person up from a seat. When strong movements are performed quickly, they are generally referred to as being powerful.

- *Flexibility*. This refers to the capacity of the joints of the human body to move through a standard range of motion or beyond. Standards are population-specific and flexibility is usually held to be greater in females than in males and is thought to decline after puberty. Gymnasts need to very flexible in the trunk, hips and shoulders. Swimmers tend to be particularly flexible in the shoulders. In every-day life flexibility of the joints is required in such activities as getting into and out of cramped spaces, such as sports cars, or reaching for something on a high shelf.

- *Body composition*. Having appropriate levels of body fat and fat-free mass are vital. High-performance athletes need appropriate levels of muscle as well as strong bones. The amount and placement of the muscle may be particular to the sport. Rugby players and throwers have large amounts of upper body musculature. Dancers will tend to have well-muscled legs, relative to other parts of the body. Some sports require participants to have less than the normal levels of body fat, particularly where the sport means transporting their own body mass. Thus runners and ball-games players will tend to be lean. Some sports such as martial arts and lightweight rowing have cate-gories of competition determined by body mass and thus extra body fat is not helpful. Outside sport, an excess of body fat increases arterial blood pressure putting a greater burden on the heart, as well as impairing flexibility and increasing the risk of conditions such as coronary heart disease and type 2 diabetes.

- *Mental health.* This is important for our general well-being as well as facilitating sports performance. This means having a realistic perception of ourselves, our body and our place within society. We need to be able to relate to others in a meaningful and constructive way and have the mental strength and determination to concentrate on things and see them through.

More components of fitness for sport

So far all of the components described are necessary in the sporting arena and for health function in everyday life. There are other components of fitness which perhaps relate more specifically to sports performance. These are:

- *Speed and quickness of movement.* Many sports require participants to be able to move quickly. The quickness of movement may be hand speed, as in boxing or in racquet sports, where racquet-head speed translates into ball or shuttlecock speed. It may also be leg speed such as in running or kicking. Speed of movement will be determined and limited by the fibre typing of the musculature involved as well as the state of training of that musculature.
- *Agility.* The ability to move quickly, change direction and maintain balance is important in all ball games and contact sports. It involves strength, speed, coordination and accurate sensory perception.
- *Balance.* This is important in all sports, whether it be sitting in a boat while rowing, balancing on a beam in gymnastics, sprinting on to the ball in soccer or sitting astride a horse as it takes a fence in equestrian sports. Balance involves strength in the core muscles of the trunk, as well as the legs. It may require the ability to shift body weight rapidly or subtly and involves inputs from the senses. It is also very important in everyday life as the ability to remain in balance reduces the incidence of falls. The elderly are more prone to falling and this, coupled with their more brittle bones, can make them particularly vulnerable.
- *Reaction time.* This refers to the time taken to respond to a given stimulus. Visual reaction time is the slowest of the response modalities, with kinaesthetic response time, where feedback from the

proprioceptors in ligaments and tendons initiates the response the fastest. Response to an auditory stimulus is faster than to a visual one. Reaction time is trainable; hence sprinters and swimmers will train by practising starts.

Fitness is essential to all, in everything we do, as it reduces the incidence of stress, illness and injury. We need different elements and types of fitness to do different things, but it is something which should not be taken for granted. Almost all elements of fitness are trainable and are affected by the ageing process.

FURTHER READING

Brown, S.J., Miller, W.C. and Eason, J.M. (2006) *Exercise Physiology: Basis for Human Movement in Health and Disease*. Philadelphia, PA: Lippincott, Williams & Wilkins.
Corbin, C., Welk, G., Corbin, W. and Welk, K. (2007) *Concepts of Fitness and Wellness: A Comprehensive Lifestyle Approach*, 7th edn. New York: McGraw Hill.

RON BUTTERLY

Growth, Maturation, Motor Development and Learning

INTRODUCTION AND DEFINITIONS

During the period young people are at school they undergo enormous changes through the processes of growth, maturation and development. Growth is a dominant biological activity during the first two decades of life. Maturation refers to the process of becoming a mature adult. Development is a much broader concept, encompassing growth, maturation, learning and experience and relates to becoming more competent in general life skills. Every young person will undergo cognitive, motor and emotional development during their time at school, all of which will have a profound effect on shaping them as a person.

Motor development can be considered as the process by which young people acquire movement patterns, skills and techniques. It is characterised by continuous modification, based on neuromuscular maturation, growth and maturation of the body, the residual effects of prior experiences and those of new motor experiences. Motor learning can be defined as a set of internal processes associated with practice or experience leading to relatively permanent changes in response capabilities.

Fundamental, general or basic motor skills and movement patterns, such as walking, running, skipping, jumping, catching, throwing, climbing and hopping are developed during the postnatal period. By the time young people enter school they will be able to perform some of the fundamental motor skills and movement patterns with some success. However, the range of individual physical competence demonstrated at the time of engagement with compulsory education will already be very broad, from those who cannot catch or throw to those who are able to demonstrate, at least some of the time, mature fundamental movement patterns through their refinement as skills and techniques. In those who are more advanced in their development, these skills and techniques may already be recognisable as the basic components necessary for high-performance adult sport.

LONGITUDINAL GROWTH STUDIES

In terms of an evidence base, the first longitudinal growth study was published in the nineteenth century, with new impetus provided by Boas around the beginning of the twentieth century, when he recognised the individual variation in the tempo of growth and was responsible for the introduction of the concept of physiological age or biological maturation, which is not the same as chronological age. Since the 1920s a series of longitudinal studies have been conducted which have continued to refine our knowledge and understanding of physical growth and maturation. The Amsterdam Growth Study constitutes a more recent example of a comprehensive longitudinal European growth study.

THE ADOLESCENT GROWTH SPURT

Generally, sex differences that influence motor development and performance are minimal before adolescence. On average girls begin their adolescent growth spurt two years before boys (at 12 and 14 years respectively), which means that, during this period, girls may be taller and heavier than their male peers. Boys do then outgrow girls in their adolescent growth spurt to attain, on average, a larger adult stature. During the early part of the growth spurt greater increases are seen in the lower limbs, followed later by an increase in trunk length and then a greater increase in muscle mass. Regional differences in growth also occur during the adolescent growth spurt, with boys producing only a slightly greater increase in calf muscle mass than girls, but nearly twice the increase in muscle mass of the arm.

Relatively minor differences in average body dimensions between girls and boys are magnified by the adolescent growth spurt, resulting in girls having broader hips and pelvis, with proportionately longer trunk length relative to leg length and an increase to an average body fat percentage of around 25 per cent. Boys are leaner, averaging around 15 per cent body fat, with greater muscle mass, broader shoulders, narrower hips, longer legs and straighter limbs. Such average differences between the sexes, coupled with a very wide range of individual differences in timing and rate of change have profound implications for motor development and physical competence. For example, given the relatively large changes in the size (of the order of 5–10 cm in height, 6–7 kg in mass in less than one year), shape and physical characteristics that change the mechanics of the movement (mass, inertia, force, torque, etc.), accomplished performers can appear clumsy and uncoordinated and may be unable to reproduce well-established and often sophisticated techniques. Individual patterns of growth and maturation therefore change the mechanical constraints placed on movement patterns and these changes require physical conditioning and then practice to re-establish skill levels, even though existing generalised motor patterns and schema may already be quite well established.

INDIVIDUAL VARIABILITY IN MOTOR DEVELOPMENT AND LEARNING

There is a strong rationale for focusing on the individual as interpretation based on average values for boys and girls can be misleading. For example, while peak height velocity may, on average, be reached at 12 years for girls and 14 years for boys, there can be up to five years' difference in the timing of such growth and similar variation in the timing and tempo of the development of secondary sex characteristics between individuals of the same sex. The parallel interactive effects of physical development with cognitive, social and emotional development that take place throughout the school years provide a strong rationale for the need for core **Physical Education** and a variety of physical activity, exercise and sports experiences throughout compulsory education, as the body and the person are continually changing throughout growth, maturation and development into a mature adult.

KEY POINTS

- Growth, maturation and motor development result in profound changes in the physical size and competence of young people throughout compulsory education, exemplified by an approximate doubling in stature between the age of two and adulthood.
- Growth, maturation and development not only impact on motor learning but also interact in a variety of complex ways with emotional, social and cognitive development.
- Biomechanical variables constantly change in magnitude as young people grow and mature, providing an unstable basis for consolidation of basic movement patterns and the development of skills and techniques.

FURTHER READING

Malina, R.M., Bouchard, C. and Bar-Or, O. (2004) *Growth, Maturation and Physical Activity*, 2nd edn. Champaign, IL: Human Kinetics.
Schmidt, R.A. and Wrisberg, C.A. (2007) *Motor Learning and Performance*, 4th edn. Champaign, IL: Human Kinetics.

CARLTON COOKE

growth, maturation, motor development and learning

PART III

INTRODUCTION

Sport and exercise pedagogy refers to the interrelated processes of **Instruction**, learning and subject matter within specific physical activity contexts. The most familiar example of pedagogy is teaching and **Learning** in **Physical education** within schools. Increasingly, pedagogy is being recognised as important in other physical activity contexts, such as sports coaching and exercise instruction. In these two latter examples, coaches and instructors play an important role in designing experiences for players and participants that result in learning, improved performance and hopefully some enjoyment as well.

Pedagogy is of central importance in sport and exercise science since there is scarcely a context where the instruction and learning of physical activity subject matter is not taking place. Schools and sports clubs offer obvious examples, as do exercise settings such as fitness clubs. There are many other contexts in which pedagogy is operating, such as after-school clubs, holiday camps and outdoor adventure challenges. Wherever people meet and interact to engage in the practice and performance of physical activities, pedagogy will be operating. It is for this reason that understanding pedagogy and its component parts is important.

In this section you will first of all learn more about physical education as the context most closely associated with sport and exercise pedagogy. You can then read about instruction, learning and **Curriculum**, the latter involving the organisation of subject matter for learning. Finally, you can read about **Assessment**. While assessment plays a formal role in some aspects of school physical education, it is also an important means of measuring the progress of learning and performance in other contexts.

DAVID KIRK

Physical Education

The meaning of physical education has been contested vigorously since it came into regular use in most English-speaking countries from the 1950s. Before the 1950s, the term physical training was more common. Some of the debates around meaning have centred on the content, teaching styles and learning that characterise physical education as a subject area in the school curriculum. Other debates have been concerned with physical education as a lifelong process of learning in the physical domain. Often these two broad approaches to physical education are presented as antagonistic to each other though, as we will see, this need not necessarily be the case. Within the context of these two broad approaches to physical education, writers have employed a number of specific strategies to determine the meaning of the concept.

The first, most common and straightforward of these strategies has been to state a definition of physical education. While definitions vary in specificity, explicitness and scope, most make links between learning in the physical domain and a range of related outcomes concerned with social skills, moral values, health, spirituality and intellectual ability. A relatively sophisticated version of a definition of physical education can be found in *The National Curriculum for England: Physical Education* which will be implemented from 2008 to 2011:

> Physical education develops pupils' physical competence and confidence, and their ability to use these to perform in a range of activities. It promotes physical skilfulness, physical development and a knowledge of the body in action. Physical education provides opportunities for pupils to be creative, competitive and to face up to different challenges as individuals and in groups and teams. It promotes positive attitudes towards active and healthy lifestyles. Pupils learn how to think in different ways to suit a wide variety of creative, competitive and challenging activities. They learn how to plan, perform and evaluate actions, ideas and performances to improve their quality and effectiveness. Through this process pupils discover their aptitudes, abilities and preferences, and make choices about how to get involved in lifelong physical activity. (QCA, 2007, www.nc.uk.net)

This definition is clearly focused on the first of the two broad approaches, understanding physical education as a subject area in the school **Curriculum**, although it does also contain some traces of the notion of physical education as a lifelong process.

While many definitions of physical education now exist, it is also widely recognised that there seems to be little consensus over which particular definition should be preferred. Part of the reason for this lack of consensus may be that, while some definitions are broad in scope like the one above, few are underpinned by a theoretical perspective.

The second strategy to identify the meaning of physical education emerged as a response to the work of educational philosophers Richard Peters and Paul Hirst in the 1960s and 1970s and sought to provide a solution to the apparent shortcoming of the definitional strategy. Peters and Hirst sought to clarify the meaning of a range of concepts, such as education, drawing broadly on Ludwig Wittgenstein's approach to language analysis. Behind their apparently disinterested analysis of concepts, the philosophers of education were seeking to identify which areas of knowledge should be included in the school curriculum and, implicitly, which should be omitted. This line of investigation had important and serious consequences for physical education. Peters' and his colleagues' analyses of education concluded that physical education could not be regarded as an educationally worthwhile activity. It therefore could not be considered part of a compulsory or core curriculum that all children should experience.

Several philosophers of physical education rose to the challenge presented by this work and they discovered many ingenious arguments with which to counter Peters' and his colleagues' conclusions. Some argued that physical education was an aesthetic activity since it included dance and movement education. Since aesthetic activities were included in Hirst's list of forms of knowledge, it was argued that physical education therefore should be part of the school core curriculum. Others suggested that competitive activities such as sports presented children with moral challenges. Since physical education includes sports, and since, according to Peters, educationally worthwhile activities are marked by a moral seriousness, they suggested that physical education should also therefore be regarded as educationally worthwhile. Taking a more radical stance, another group of philosophers proposed that physical education was a form of practical knowledge in its own right, and deserved to be included in the curriculum on that basis.

This second philosophical strategy certainly introduced a measure of intellectual rigour and theoretical sophistication to the task of understanding the meaning of physical education. While some of the ideas generated by conceptual analysis have influenced more recent theorising about physical education's place in the school curriculum, such as Margaret Whitehead's notion of 'physical literacy', by and large this great volume of philosophical literature did little to produce a consensus over the meaning of physical education, particularly in terms of which definition to prefer.

A third strategy began to emerge in the 1970s just as the language analysis approach of the philosophers was beginning to lose its momentum. Research in the sociology of knowledge, particularly as it began to take shape in the work of writers such as M.F.D. Young, Basil Bernstein and Pierre Bourdieu, put forward the radical proposition that the school curriculum is an example of the social organisation of knowledge. This proposition suggested that, rather than having intrinsic worth that transcends societies and historical epochs, as Peters for example had argued, the school curriculum is the product of a range of social forces, involving the exercise of power and embodying particular values and preferences.

The full significance of this insight was brought out in the work of curriculum historians such as Herbert Kliebard and Ivor Goodson. Goodson suggested that school subjects and university disciplines do not evolve. Instead, they follow trajectories of popularity and perceived importance through struggles between vying groups and individuals. These groups and individuals actively contest each others' preferences and seek to establish their own preferences for particular versions of school knowledge, either at the overall level of the school curriculum or in relation to specific subject areas.

The key message of this line of research was that, if we wish to understand the meaning of a subject area such as physical education (or geography or mathematics), we must study what people do in the name of that subject area. In other words, a subject is defined by its practices. When we apply this proposition to physical education, we discover that the practice of physical education is often quite different from the various aspirational definitions produced by government policy makers.

Contemporary research on the practice of physical education in England suggests that for children aged 5–14, the majority of time in the school curriculum is devoted to practising sports skills (such as the lateral pass in rugby, the push pass in hockey, the lay-up shot in basketball, etc.) and to a lesser extent participating in games and sports. Children also spend some time learning to swim, to perform gymnastics feats and to dance. This research suggests that the majority of teaching follows a traditional, didactic approach, where the teacher directs lessons, and a task-based approach, where pupils work at a 'station' in a small group for a defined period of time before moving on the next station. Despite mounting pressure since the early 1980s to create more time for health-related exercise activities, this contemporary research suggests that skill-learning and performing games and sports continue to dominate school programmes, particularly for children in the 8–14 age range.

Post-14, physical education becomes a highly successful subject area for study towards GCSE and A Level awards in England, a trend that can also be observed in countries such as Australia, New Zealand and Scotland. Sports leadership awards and vocational qualifications in sport and leisure have seen similar increases in uptake in the UK. GCSE physical education mixes participation in physical activities such as games and sports, swimming, gymnastics and dance with classroom-based studies of, for example, exercise, nutrition and **Principles of Training**. At A Level, the physical activity content is reduced considerably and pupils study topics such as sports sociology, exercise physiology and sports psychology. Sports leadership awards are often integrated into curricular physical education programmes.

The dominance of sport-related content in contemporary physical education programmes in England and elsewhere runs counter to definitions of the subject area offered by the National Curriculum and to the advocacy of researchers who seek to improve the quality and equity of current programmes, particularly in terms of provision for girls, young disabled people and ethnic minority groups, each of whom it is claimed is disadvantaged by the dominant form of physical education. Curriculum history research reveals some insights into why the way of practising physical education just described persists in the face of opposition from groups of professionals and researchers.

It was mentioned at the beginning of this section that the term physical education began to supersede that of physical training in England and other English-speaking countries after the Second World War, and through the 1950s and 1960s began to be commonly used to describe the subject area and the educational process. The shift from the word training to education signalled an allied shift in thinking, from a physical, functional and mainly scientific approach, to a whole-person, arts-based approach. Leading this development were the female physical educators who as a group had dominated physical training in schools from the 1890s until the 1950s. The females' view of physical education was strongly influenced by their replacement of free-standing exercises such as Dano-Swedish gymnastics with a form of movement education influenced by Rudolf Laban (among others). The women teachers saw physical education as a creative, aesthetic subject area.

This view was not shared by their male colleagues, however, who entered the physical education profession in increasing numbers from the 1950s. While they also preferred the term physical education to physical training, the education dimension for the men was developed through playing games and sports that until the 1940s had mainly been restricted to private schools in England. They argued that games and sports were excellent media through which to develop physical skills, and also social and moral attributes such as cooperation, leadership, deferred gratification, competitiveness and appropriate levels of aggression.

These different views of female and male teachers divided the physical education profession throughout the 1960s and 1970s in England. Such was the depth of disagreement between the women and men that physical education was and, in some places in England remains today, one of the few subject areas in the school curriculum with separate female and male departments, with separate programmes and single-sex lessons for boys and girls and, up until the mid-1980s, separate training colleges for men and women student teachers. While distinctively different programmes continue to survive within the context of the National Curriculum Physical Education (NCPE) in England, the arts-focused female perspective gradually lost ground to the games and sports-oriented male perspective prior to the establishment of the NCPE in the early 1990s.

In other parts of the English-speaking world such as Australia and the USA, co-educational physical education had been in place since the early 1970s, in contrast to the situation in England. However, in these countries also the games-oriented male perspective dominates over the arts-based female perspective. The gender conflict that was a significant driving force behind the practice of physical education in the 1950s to 1970s has been submerged by the dominance of the games and sports perspective.

This fact in itself provides some clues to the resilience to change of the games and sports practices that currently dominate physical education. The qualities that participation in games and sports is claimed to develop – courage, leadership, cooperation and competitiveness – together with the fact that it can promote health and combat obesity – have made the issue a powerful ideological tool when mobilised by politicians and other groups with vested interests in promoting games and sports. Studies have investigated how politicians from Margaret Thatcher to John Major and Tony Blair have coopted sporting imagery to promote their own political agendas. These studies confirm that physical education has been and remains a contested concept.

FURTHER READING

Morgan, W.J. (2006) 'Philosophy and physical education', in D. Kirk, D. Macdonald and M.O'Sullivan (eds), *Handbook of Physical Education*. London: Sage. pp. 97–108. Qualifications & Curriculum Authority (2007) *The National Curriculum for England: Physical Education*. London: QCA. (See also http:// www.nc.uk.net.)

DAVID KIRK
TONI O'DONOVAN

Instruction

The term instruction is most commonly used in the USA. We enlist it here because it is a useful way of including teaching, coaching, and leadership activities in a range of sites in which sport and other physical activities are practised and learned. We suggest that the practices of teaching, coaching and leadership have much in common, with any differences arising through the setting and its particular features. Having made this point, it should be noted that the majority of research on instruction in physical activity settings has been carried out on teaching Physical Education in school.

The earliest forms of instruction in physical education were dominated by a singular approach where pupils closely followed the procedures outlined by their teacher. The shift in philosophy towards a more child-centred approach to education in the 1950s led to changes in methods of instruction. Throughout the 1950s and 1960s the dominant conception of physical education shifted, with an increasing range of goals and objectives identified for physical education in a variety of domains. New ways for teachers to instruct pupils in physical education began to emerge at this time, focused on child-centred instruction. Over half a century later the conception of instruction has gone through numerous cycles of development and the range of styles, strategies and models from which teachers draw has expanded dramatically.

In sports coaching, investigations into coach behaviour grew from this educational foundation where analysis of instruction was perceived by some to have increased legitimacy, as the instructional behaviour of coaches was viewed as being more directly related to outcomes, such as win/loss. Many authors stress the importance of such analysis in establishing an empirical base for a future 'science' of coaching, especially as related to coach behaviour. Undoubtedly, the studies conducted to date have yielded insights that have contributed greatly to the body of knowledge in sports coaching.

Since a landmark study in the 1970s examining UCLA's basketball coach John Wooden's coaching behaviour, certain behaviours do consistently permeate the findings of behavioural studies and, hence, reveal a commonality that cannot be ignored. Particularly evident here are high levels of instruction. Arguably, a high level of instruction is a prerequisite for effective coaching. Indeed, instructional feedback, encouragement and positive reinforcement are suggested as crucial behaviours for coaches. While there remains little doubt regarding the efficacy of these behaviours, there are no global rules as to their application. It would seem that the link between instruction and coaching effectiveness relates more to context of use and quality rather than sheer quantity alone.

The most detailed analysis of instruction was first undertaken in 1966 by Mosston, who described a spectrum of instructional styles in terms of the extent to which the pupils or teacher are involved in making decisions about the learning tasks. He conceptualised a unified series of styles based on the control of decision making in the class. The 'Spectrum' incorporates ten landmark styles on a continuum, with the teacher-led approach (formal and direct) at one extreme and a much more open-ended and student-centred style (informal and indirect), with the teacher acting mainly in a facilitatory role at the other. The Spectrum offers a range of options to teachers that can accommodate students' diverse learning styles and meet the learning intentions of a teaching session more accurately. Although this work is open to criticism, it has become the most widely adopted framework in initial teacher education. Despite the widespread influence of Mosston's instructional styles, research into instruction in physical education indicates that, typically, students continue to be taught based on content and subject area, with teachers teaching, for example, basketball skills, in a particular order rather than basing instruction on the outcomes and goals for a unit of activity.

Simultaneously, a research programme emerged around the notion of effective teaching, with the aim of determining which teacher behaviours correlated with student engagement and achievement. A focus developed on examining which instructional strategies, such as the use of open or closed tasks, demonstration and questioning techniques, resulted in an increase in student **Learning**. However, despite the attempts to delineate which teacher behaviour results in improved learning, debates still rage about which strategies are most effective, for example, the introduction of streaming, banding and setting as alternatives to mixed ability grouping.

Over the past 30 years instructional models have emerged to respond to the need for comprehensive and unifying programmes that can help teachers see a bigger picture for ways to teach physical education. Metzler (2000) argues that, in contrast to the instructional strategies or styles suitable for only particular learning activities, a model is designed to be used for an entire unit of instruction and includes all of the planning design, implementation and assessment functions of that unit, utilising multiple methods, strategies and styles. Models such as 'Teaching Games for Understanding' and 'Sport Education' have gained in popularity over the past two decades.

'Sport Education' is a curriculum and instruction model designed for delivery in physical education programmes. The model was originally developed and introduced in 1986 by Daryl Siedentop, who was concerned that, despite sport being the key content area of physical education, young people were not experiencing authentic versions of sport and the associated sporting culture. It is intended to provide young people with more authentic and enjoyable sports experiences than those typically seen in physical education classes. The three major goals that guide Sport Education are for students to become competent, literate and enthusiastic players (Siedentop, 1994).

The basic structure of 'Sport Education' is adapted from the familiar model of organised sport. Siedentop (1994) identified six key features that make sport special (seasons, team affiliation, formal competition, culminating events, record keeping and festivity). Students participate as members of persisting teams in seasons that last approximate 16 to 20 lessons, which is longer than a usual physical education unit. They take an active role in their own sports experience by serving in varied and realistic roles that we see in authentic sports settings, such as captains, coaches, trainers, statisticians, officials, publicists and members of a sports council. This gives the students a broader experience of sport as they learn the skills, responsibilities and roles that are associated with organised sport. Central to this model is the aim of educating students in all aspects of a sports culture. Persisting teams are encouraged to develop affiliation through the selection of team names, logos and chants as they work through a season of formal competition, culminating in a festival. The students are recognised and rewarded for fair play, improvement and the roles that they adopted during the season at the culminating festival.

The 'Sport Education' model relies extensively on cooperative learning strategies and the teaching styles involved lie at the student-centred end of Mosston's Spectrum of Teaching Styles, thus allowing students to take responsibility for many of the decisions within the season.

Increasingly, physical education is being tasked with a growing range of goals and objectives in a broad variety of domains. As a result it has become apparent that teachers cannot instruct in the same manner all the time, or be limited to particular instructional methods, strategies or models. To engage young people in physical education, teachers are required to refresh their teaching, drawing on a range of exciting, new and effective ways of instructing in the varied locations in which they teach and with increasing use of the technology now available in schools.

FURTHER READING

Metzler, M. (2000) *Instructional Models for Physical Education*. Boston, MA: Allyn & Bacon.

Siedentop, D. (1994) 'Introduction to sport education', in D. Siedentop (ed.), *Sport Education: Quality PE through Positive Sport Experiences*. Champaign, IL: Human Kinetics. pp. 3–16.

TONI O'DONOVAN
CHRIS CUSHION

Learning

Learning is a process that results in a change in behaviour, an improvement in performance, in the acquisition of knowledge, in a disposition to act in particular ways. Behind this bland definition, a brief exploration of research around this concept reveals that learning is complex and multidimensional, taking different shapes and bringing different phenomena into play according to the theoretical perspective of the researcher.

The earliest research on learning in **Physical Education** and sport settings, dating from the late 1970s through to the early 1990s, focused on the amount of time and the frequency of practice as the key to understanding learning. Researchers suggested that the more time a learner spent engaged in appropriate activities, and the more often those activities were practised, the more effective learning was likely to result. Both time and frequency of practice together present what researchers called 'opportunities to learn'. They adapted a construct from classroom research – Academic Learning Time (ALT) – to express this notion of the time learners spend engaging in appropriate physical education activities (ALT-PE). Studies using this construct found that there is a relationship between ALT-PE and motor competence, but only early in the learning process. Once a learner had moved beyond the novice stage, more time did not necessarily result in better performance, but instead performance plateaued and even declined. Nevertheless, they discovered that lower-skilled learners had lower ALT-PE scores in physical education classes than higher-skilled learners, as did secondary school-aged girls than boys and young disabled people than able-bodied. They also discovered that levels of ALT-PE varied according to activity type, so that it was easier to gain higher scores on closed skills and techniques such as a golf swing than it was on open skills such as playing basketball. They discovered that what teachers do in terms of managing the learning environment does make a difference to students' opportunities to learn.

This insight, that the process of teaching could impact on the product of student learning, was an important contribution to understanding learning. However, by the early 1980s, researchers were pointing out that this 'process–product' approach was too simplistic. For one thing research had tended to focus too much on teachers rather than learners and the environments in which teaching and learning took place. And for another, the process–product approach assumed that teaching *causes* learning. Eminent educational researcher Walter Doyle argued that, on the contrary, student behaviour often influences what teachers do. He argued that other factors impact on learning in addition to teacher behaviour and he developed the 'classroom ecology' approach in which learning was studied as it occurred naturally. This allowed researchers to focus on the many aspects of the learning environment that could influence learning. One aspect of this environment was the student social system. Researchers found that students came to physical education classes with two goals in mind, to socialise, and to pass the course or, at least, keep the teacher happy. One study discovered that some students had learned to appear to be 'busy, happy and good', thereby keeping the teacher happy, while engaging in social activity with peers. Another study found, in a similar fashion, that some less skilled students had learned to become 'competent bystanders', appearing to be actively engaged in appropriate tasks but in fact avoiding engagement whenever possible. This line of research uncovered the possibility that there was what Philip Jackson famously called a 'hidden curriculum' operating in all classrooms. The hidden curriculum concept has since been deployed by researchers to show that students learn more than just the formal curriculum of their lessons.

Some of the earliest research on learning motor skills dating from the 1950s proposed that cognition was an important part of learning physical skills. However, it was not until much later that educational researchers began to take cognition seriously in understanding learning in physical education and sport. Researchers using information processing as an analogy for human learning found that learning to perform a physical skill such as a soccer pass involved three actions, perceiving, deciding and moving. Perceiving involved searching the environment for information – such as the whereabouts of team mates and opponents – and selecting information needed to decide what to do. Deciding to pass involves a choice between other options such as dribbling or shooting. The actual execution of the movement, the observable behaviour of kicking the ball, was the component of the skill that ALT-PE researchers had tended to focus on. This meant that they tended not to account for the importance of the cognitive processes of perceiving and deciding when applying their research findings to improve student learning.

More recently, since the 1990s, researchers have applied the concept of cognitive mediation to better understand learning. Although there exists a range of theories of cognition, most have in common the idea that learning requires students to engage actively with the learning environment. They have discovered that in physical education classes, students presented with the same task often respond differently. Their varying interpretations of a task are influenced, among other things, by their different experiences prior to encountering the task. For example, one distinguishing characteristic of expert performers in sport is that they make more appropriate decisions about what to do compared with novices, since their prior experience has prepared them to identify which information within the environment of, say, a soccer game, is most relevant and important. Studies of learning using the notion of cognitive mediation have shown that students' perceptions of their own competence can impact on their ability to learn, while learner perceptions and interpretations affect motivation, attention and concentration. Research has discovered naïve conceptions and misconceptions about for example the relationships between exercise, health and body shapes, and about game tactics, each of which influences learning.

More recent theoretical developments since the late 1990s have continued to yield increasingly sophisticated insights into learning. Building on the notions from cognitive mediation that learning is an active process of engagement with subject matter within an environment, and that learners construct knowledge on the basis of their prior experiences, constructivist theories add that learning is socially constructed. By this they mean that much learning takes place in social settings, such as classrooms, and that we learn from others, such as peers, teachers, parents and so on. Researchers using situated learning theories have added that cognition and learning are socially constructed in the sense that they are distributed across the individual, subject matter and the environment rather than contained within each. For example, in learning to pass the ball in rugby, knowing when to pass is crucial and, for beginners, often hard to learn. The player passing the ball must commit their opponent to contact but be able to make the pass before being tackled. In order to learn this skill, the cognitive demands of perception and decision making are offloaded onto the environment by, for example, requiring the pass and tackle to take place in a 5 m × 10 m zone. Other examples of this concept of distributed cognition involving manipulating the learning environment include modifications to the task (throw–catch tennis without a racquet), modifications to equipment (a short-handled tennis racquet and soft ball), and modifications to the playing area (a long, narrow or short, wide court).

Further developments of situated learning theory have shown that learning occurs not just in social settings but also in wider communities of practice. Moving from the role of novice to expert within a particular physical activity community such as that of rock climbers or basketball players is akin to an apprenticeship to become a baker or a motor mechanic. While there is subject matter to be mastered, there are also in each of these cases customs to be observed, values to be internalised, and modes of interaction between community members to be learned.

Learning to become a motor mechanic or a rock climber will involve both formal and informal opportunities to learn. Crucially, situated learning theories suggest that learning occurs most effectively when experiences appear authentic and meaningful to the learner and important to the activities of other members of the community. Situated learning research is revealing that learning in physical education and sport is informed by popular physical cultural practices such as media sport and fitness culture. In this context, the learning of people young and old shapes and is shaped by their embodied self-identities, creating tastes, values and dispositions.

FURTHER READING

Rovegno, I. (2006) 'Situated perspectives on learning', in D. Kirk, D. Macdonald and M. O'Sullivan (eds), *Handbook of Physical Education*. London: Sage. pp. 262–74.
Solmon, M. (2006) 'Learner cognition', in D. Kirk, D. Macdonald and M. O'Sullivan (eds), *Handbook of Physical Education*. London: Sage. pp. 226–41.

DAVID KIRK

Curriculum

Curriculum refers to a range of educational experiences, planned and unplanned, associated with student **Learning**. Content is only part of the educational experience. **Physical Education** is distinguishable from other curricular areas by its focus on **The Body** and movement, seeking to build on previously learned movement skills through participation in a diverse range of physical activity-related experiences. The physical education curriculum is concerned with instilling a desire for, and encouraging lifelong involvement in, physical activity. Most physical education curricula constitute a rationale, aims, objectives, areas of study/range of practical activities (e.g. dance, games), learning outcomes and assessing student learning, hoping to produce 'physically educated' young people. There is consensus that the physical education curriculum applies a holistic approach to the concept of physical activity for school-aged students, providing opportunities to:

- enhance physical, mental, emotional and social development;
- develop physical creativity, competence and confidence to perform a variety of physical activities;
- examine human movement from different key perspectives;
- work as individuals, with partners, in groups and as part of a team, in both competitive and non-competitive situations;
- encourage an appreciation of physical activities and promote positive attitudes towards establishing and sustaining an active and healthy lifestyle.

The work of Catherine Ennis discusses how curriculum reflects an educational philosophy, illustrating that teachers' **Expertise** in the subject area and beliefs about best practice inform the way in which the curriculum is delivered. Ennis's work focuses on value orientations in curricular decision making and explores the educational beliefs of physical education teachers – discipline mastery, learning process, self-actualisation, social responsibility and justice and ecological integration. Ennis examines how each reflect teachers' educational beliefs about what students should learn, how they should engage in the learning process, and how learning should be assessed. The ability to teach physical education curriculum in a manner consistent with value orientations is aided or constrained by the complex school environment.

International barriers to the provision and delivery of the physical education curriculum and to effecting the implementation of developments in physical education curriculum are well documented. They include inadequate facilities and equipment, shortage of time on the curriculum (marked reduction in time allocated to physical education in the upper secondary school), inadequate physical education training for primary teachers, inappropriate staffing levels and a lack of sufficient and appropriate professional development for physical education teachers. These factors interact and addressing one constraint in isolation will not necessarily lead to enduring change in the physical education curriculum.

The extent to which the delivery of a physical education curriculum is enforced varies considerably. In England, physical education is statutory but with no time requirement stipulated. In some countries, schools are required to offer a programme of physical education to all students with a minimum time allocation for physical education stipulated. In other countries schools 'should' offer a physical education programme within a 'suggested' time allocation. In others, physical education has been removed from the curriculum or further reductions in physical education curriculum time allocation have been pursued.

One similarity that is evident across countries delivering a physical education curriculum is the amount of time invested in teaching games, usually at the expense of other activity areas. Physical education curriculum has tended to focus on discrete activities such as soccer and basketball. Michael Metzler, Jacalyn Lund and Deborah Tannehill present curricular models as an attempt to introduce a medium through which teachers can teach towards learning goals (refocusing attention from the particular activity), communicate such learning goals to students and increase the opportunities students can experience by designing the physical education curriculum on specific themes and different pedagogical principles. Such models include Personal and Social Responsibility, Sport Education, and Teaching Games for Understanding.

By offering extra-curricular activities that are available to all students wishing to be involved, physical education contributes to the 'extended curriculum'. That is, curriculum that enriches the social and cultural life of the school and is separate to the more formal curriculum pursued throughout the school day. Such activities are not necessarily part of a teacher's contractual agreement though many teachers may choose to coach or supervise on a voluntary basis. By its unique nature, physical education can also contribute towards 'whole-school curriculum'. That is, promoting a shared responsibility from everyone in the school to support the importance of active living, health and well-being, priorities that significantly contribute to the life of a school.

The National Curriculum in England applies to students of compulsory school age and is organised on the basis of four key stages:

- key stage 1 covers ages 5 to 7 (Years 1 to 2);
- key stage 2 covers ages 7 to 11 (Years 3 to 6);
- key stage 3 covers ages 11 to 14 (Years 7 to 9); and
- key stage 4 covers ages 14 to 16 (Years 10 to 11).

The new secondary National Curriculum in England introduces changes to the curriculum at key stages 3 and 4. While maintaining the discipline of subjects, e.g. art and design, English and physical education, the new secondary National Curriculum allows sufficient flexibility for schools to design their own locally determined curriculum to meet their learners' needs, capabilities and aspirations. It is envisaged that the curriculum should enable all young people to become

1 successful learners who enjoy learning, make progress and achieve;
2 confident individuals who are able to live safe, healthy and fulfilling lives; and
3 responsible citizens who make a positive contribution to society.

For each school subject at each school stage there exists a 'programme of study' and 'attainment target'.

The revised programmes of study at key stages 3 and 4 focus on key concepts and processes that underlie each subject rather than on prescribed subject content. Four key concepts that underpin the study of physical education are listed in the physical education programme of study for key stage 3 and key stage 4. These are competence, performance, creativity and healthy, active lifestyles. The key processes sections in the programmes of study highlight the essential skills that learners need in order to make progress and achieve in each subject. The five essential skills and processes in physical education are listed as:

1 developing skills in physical activity;
2 making and applying decisions;
3 developing physical and mental capacity;
4 evaluating and improving; and
5 making informed choices about healthy, active lifestyles.

The programmes of study also outline the breadth of the subject on which teachers should draw when teaching the key concepts and key processes and also curriculum opportunities that are integral to pupils' learning and enhance their engagement with the concepts, processes and content of the subject.

The attainment target sets out the knowledge, skills and understanding that students of different abilities and maturities are expected to have achieved by completion of each key stage. Attainment targets consist of eight level descriptions (describing the type and range of performance that students working at that level should characteristically demonstrate) of increasing difficulty and there is a description for exceptional performance above level 8. The level descriptions in physical education indicate progression in the aspects set out in the programme of study and provide the basis for making judgements about students' performance at the end of key stages 1, 2 and 3. There is an expected attainment for the majority of students on completion of each key stage.

Physical education is being inextricably linked to the promotion of positive attitudes towards establishing and sustaining an active and healthy lifestyle. Consequently, the school physical education curriculum is encouraged to more closely align with opportunities available to young people to be involved in school sport and sport in the community. In England, the Physical Education, School Sport and Club Links (PESSCL) strategy was launched in 2002 to transform physical education and school sport. In December 2004, the UK Prime Minister announced the Government's long-term aim to offer all children four hours of sport a week by 2010, arising from at least two hours' curriculum physical education and an additional two to three hours beyond the school day, delivered by a range of school, community and club providers. While such an ambition supports physical education as a discrete curriculum area, there continues to be interest and debate in the relationship between physical education, sport, health and recreation. As support for physical activity to be promoted through a coordinated school health programme, with links established between the school, family and community increases, it may be deemed that school curricula alone cannot develop an active lifestyle. In fact, school physical education may be creating a social vacuum of physical activity where the expectations to become involved in, and maintain, an active lifestyle resides solely with physical education. If physical education is to sustain a place within the school curriculum, it is imperative that it engages with those forces in operation outside the school that shape the substance of what is taught through the physical education curriculum. The future role and survival of the physical education curriculum remains uncertain.

FURTHER READING

Lund, J. and Tannehill, D. (2005) *Standards-based Physical Education Curriculum Development*. Boston, MA: Jones and Bartlett.
Penney, D. (2006) 'Curriculum construction and change', in D. Kirk, D. Macdonald and M. O'Sullivan (eds), *Handbook of Physical Education*. London: Sage. pp. 565–79.

ANN MACPHAIL

curriculum

In recent decades, assessment has emerged as one of the most problematic and contested domains within educational arenas in general and in the realm of **Physical Education** in particular. In the wider world of education, assessment, synonymous with high-stakes examinations, is being used to facilitate selection and demonstrate central administration accountability. This emphasis has brought the concept of assessment and more specifically examinations into disrepute in some quarters. Within the physical education arena itself, the conspicuous incompatibility of some of the assessment arrangements in place with the nature and purpose of physical education has caused unease among physical education researchers and practitioners alike.

For all of these problems, the power of assessment and its potential to positively affect **Curriculum** and **Pedagogy** has long been recognised by writers such as Basil Bernstein and David Hargreaves. Therefore, it is unsurprising that, against the backdrop of the high-stakes assessments and their associated problems, there has been growing interest in alternative approaches to measuring and promoting **Learning**, spawning a movement towards more authentic forms of assessment. It is this evolution in how assessment is conceived and practised and its implications for physical education that forms the focus of this entry.

Assessment is considered to be integral to the teaching and learning process, yet systematic forms of assessment did not feature as a source of concern in the early stages of the subject's existence within education curricula. The reasons for this lie partly in the manner in which the subject was initially conceived and construed within education and partly in the nature of the subject itself. The early conceptions of physical education as physical training and its strong association with drill obscured the need for assessment. As the subject evolved, teachers began to employ what is loosely termed as 'informal observation' to form judgements of what students learn 'in', 'through' and 'about' physical education. It remains the mode of assessment most widely practised outside examination contexts; it occurs in normal teaching situations; is ongoing by nature; and its outcomes are normally represented in the school report. However, there are a number of concerns regarding its use.

It is difficult to form judgements about learning in physical education given the transitory nature of performances that leave no permanent record. Consequently, student performances are assessed on a tenuous basis with little conscious organisation or interpretation. When translated into school-report format, these assessments have been found to be preoccupied with student attitude and behaviour, effort, participation, dress, attendance and sportsmanship and avoid any reference to universalistic values that judge all students by the same criteria. In short, physical education teachers demonstrate themselves to be more concerned with student compliance than with learning.

There are contextual constraints particular to physical education, which further hinder assessment practice. It is acknowledged to be extremely difficult for teachers to make precise observational assessments while attending to the necessary safety and organisational considerations when dealing with up to 30 students actively participating in a lesson. Assessment adds to what for many teachers is an already heavy workload, entailing a significant number of classes of large size, amplified by discipline problems in some instances. To further frustrate their efforts, they have to operate in contexts that allow them limited time for the teaching of a subject, which by definition is time-consuming.

Within the wider educational arena, assessment for the purposes of monitoring standards has been adopted as a government priority in many developed countries, an application attributable in the main to motives attached to control and accountability. Physical education has not remained immune to this influence and in fact the trend towards formal state examinations has been actively supported by physical education teachers at grassroots level. Those who have researched this phenomenon found that teachers' justifications for offering examinable forms of physical education to their students had more to do with a desire for status and its associated benefits rather than with the promotion of the educational values attributable to the subject. This preoccupation can be regarded as a reaction to the marginality of the subject within an education system oriented towards academic achievement.

While examinable forms of physical education have increased at an exponential rate in America, Australia and Britain in recent decades, there are those who have overviewed this trend with caution and concern. Some regard the dissection of knowledge associated with physical education into practical and theoretical components for the purposes of formal assessment, with each being assessed independently of the other, as inappropriate. Practical knowledge in these contexts is measured via

assessment

achievement tests, observational inventories, checklists and rating scales while theoretical knowledge is assessed by the more conventional method of written tests. It is argued that these approaches fail to address what students might be learning in and through physical education. In addition, they fail to address the obvious paradox in the form of the physically gifted performer who is academically challenged.

Formal assessment of physical education within the framework of externally developed, standardised tests that monitor student progress, exhibits all the hallmarks of the limitations imposed by high-stakes examinations evident across the curriculum. Within these arrangements, validity is compromised in favour of reliability and an emphasis on the readily observable and measurable at the expense of equally valuable but less easily assessed components. This tendency in assessment leads some to argue that the unique value of physical education in developing physical literacy and in encouraging lifelong participation in physical activity is subordinated to the dominating need for comparability of results.

On a more general note, formal assessment presents a number of additional challenges. Its formal nature requires that it occur temporally and spatially away from the point of learning, thereby limiting opportunities for the outcomes to inform future learning. On a practical level, it is regarded as time-consuming and can detract from the already limited teaching time available to physical education. Formal assessment is deemed to emphasise extrinsic forms of motivation and limits the potential for those that are intrinsic and necessary for lifelong involvement in physical activity. The public nature of the assessment can be, for some, demotivating and can also generate labelling of a negative kind, discouraging efforts to improve performance. The sum of these concerns has prompted physical educators to seek out and develop more valid and effective forms of assessment that are true to the educational values inherent in physical education.

As has been highlighted throughout, many of the issues raised here are not unique to physical education, but form part of a more widespread disaffection with traditional modes of assessment across all curriculum areas. There is consensus regarding the need for change, prompting efforts to improve the efficiency of assessment and limit its undesirable side-effects. The product is a re-conceptualisation of assessment that focuses on its capacity to promote learning, as distinct from simply measuring it. This has led to the development of alternative assessment practices known variously as 'authentic assessment', 'instructional assessment', and 'assessment for learning' (AfL), probably most comprehensively defined by the UK-based Assessment Reform Group (2002) as

> the process of seeking and interpreting evidence for use by learners and their teachers to decide where the learners are in their learning, where they need to go and how best to get there.

Implicit in this re-conceptualisation of assessment are a number of key principles relating to pedagogic practice.

The first relates to the inclusion of formative assessment as an integral part of classroom practice. Research by Paul Black and Dylan Wiliam has highlighted the importance of assessment that is ongoing and incorporated with teaching and learning rather than that which forms a bolt-on element to the programme. Assessment deployed in this way informs and directs the teaching and learning process rather than representing a procedure at the end of instruction directed judgementally towards the student.

The second principle centres on the use of feedback. In this context it is important to establish the desired goal, to identify the present position and to find the means of closing the gap between the two. Particular emphasis is given to qualitative forms of feedback, which focus on constructive criticism and individualised comment rather than the use of praise or grades. Also, feedback should be specific, relate to the needs of the student and be relayed in simple terms, ideally as soon as possible after the task has been completed and while the student has opportunity to apply the feedback to their learning.

Third, this form of assessment requires the adoption of a divergent approach to teaching employing a constructivist view of learning. Openness and flexibility characterise such an approach. Students are informed of the learning goals at the outset. This might be done verbally, through a video or demonstration. This creates a situation where teachers and students can be partners in the educational process. Within this context, students are required to be active agents in their learning and as such, assume greater responsibility in monitoring their own progress. Consequently, the use of self-assessment and peer assessment, in consultation with the teacher, is encouraged. Use of these forms of assessment is regarded as a pedagogical choice, based on trust representing an organisational solution to the workload problems presented by 'teacher-only' assessment approaches.

The fourth principle stipulates that assessment be authentic, requiring that it be true to the context in which knowledge is to be applied.

Therefore, if physical activity is central to physical education, then, it follows that authentic assessment should focus on physical activity. It also follows that, if we want students to be able to apply their knowledge and skills in new situations and to evaluate their own and others' performance, tasks that embody these attributes must form part of the assessment process.

The powerful argument that can be made in support of assessment for learning is that the research has consistently demonstrated that strengthening its practice produces substantial learning gains, with particular benefits for low achievers. This resonates with both teachers and researchers who recognise the close alignment of the assessment for learning principles with the core educational values implicit in physical education. The increasing centrality of assessment for learning within educational policy marks a radical change in how assessment is viewed and practised. That can only be a good thing for physical education.

FURTHER READING

Assessment Reform Group (2002) *Assessment for Learning: Research-based Principles to Guide Classroom Practice*. See http://arg.educ.cam.ac.uk/publications.html.

Hay, P.J. (2006) 'Assessment for learning in physical education', in D. Kirk, D. Macdonald and M. O'Sullivan (eds), *Handbook of Physical Education*. London: Sage. pp. 321–5.

MARY O'FLAHERTY

PART IV

Psychology

INTRODUCTION

Sport and exercise psychology applies across the lifecycle and explores the psychological responses to the experience of sport or exercise. It is a core discipline for all who study in these domains. Further, it is fundamental to anyone interested in understanding behaviour and perhaps intervening to effect behaviour change, whether applied to high-level sport or to regular involvement in an active lifestyle. The area also addresses elements that make sport or exercise opportunities, and/or the consequences of involvement, seem positive or negative and that lead to (dis)engagement.

In many senses psychology is a fundamental science, having a reach into the other areas within this book, including **Pedagogy**. Without wishing to claim primacy for one area over another, we suggest that psychological issues represent one of a number of important influences that operate within given contexts.

The section begins with an orientation to the key theoretical areas within psychology. From there content is arranged to relate to core areas within sport and exercise psychology that students will encounter in their first undergraduate year, whether they are studying coaching, sports science, **Physical Education** or sport development. Specifically, these address **Motivation, Adherence**, Mental health, Emotion and affect, **Coping in Sport, Expertise, Leaders and Leadership** and **Communication**.

Jim McKenna

psychology

95

Motivation

Motivation has traditionally been defined as the direction and intensity of effort, meaning that we can choose whether or not to direct energy to a given task and how much we are willing to give. In this sense motivation attempts to explain why we behave the way we do. Researchers have adopted a number of different theoretical perspectives to understand the motivation for individual involvement in sport and exercise. The contemporary perspectives of Self-Determination Theory (SDT) and Social Cognitive Theory (SCT) provide the focus for this entry.

Being motivated or having the ability to motivate others can be seen as one key to success in sport and exercise. Identifying what motivates us and how to sustain that motivation continues to challenge psychologists as well as practitioners like coaches and teachers. On the one hand we can display the trait of being a 'motivated person' with high energy and interest in all activities. Alternatively, we may adopt the state of becoming motivated within a specific setting in response to what is happening there, and/or by enlisting specific intra- or interpersonal skills to alter our experience (or our perception) of what those activities mean to us. To determine the factors which most influence our motivation it is important to understand that the operative forces influence one another, i.e. they are reciprocally deterministic. In effect, motivation reflects the interaction of predispositions (including abilities and automated cognitive responses), skills to function in a specific setting and within tasks, the responsiveness of the social environment to meet individual and collective needs and biological capacity to meet imposed demands.

Motivational profiles adapt with age, following developmental markers. In childhood and adolescence, concepts of effort, ability, task difficulty and fate become refined as we learn to explain cause and effect. These explanatory patterns have important motivational implications and are profoundly influenced by how individuals understand their environment, circumstances and skills. As individuals age and acquire more experience, they develop different opinions and reasons for taking part in activity and sport. This may also help to explain age-related drop-out (e.g. competitive contact-based team sports) or adoption (e.g. golf, tennis or bowls). Decision Balance Theory holds that we act according to the balance of pros and cons that we foresee for a particular course of action within our wider lives and the likelihood of meeting success within any new behavioural options. Other approaches place particular value on the dominant motives for involvement; whether they are gain- or avoidance-based. A gain-based motive might be to learn a skill, demonstrate superiority over others or to be with friends. Enjoyment is central to these positive aspects of motivation within sport and exercise. In contrast, an aversive motive might be to avoid further injury, or to stave off worries about disease or ill health.

Contemporary perspectives have tended to understand motivation according to the nature of the environment in which sport or exercise is undertaken. For example, in Achievement Goal Theory two concepts explain individual and group styles of engagement. First, there is the role of goals and cognition; for example, if an individual's goal is to get fit and the individual believes that this requires regular gym attendance, then they are likely to attend. Second, competence and success play an important role. In this understanding, the major goals of individuals are to feel successful and to acquire some form of competence, which emphasises that practitioners ensure ample opportunities to experience positive feedback on performance. The enjoyment that results from feeling competent builds self-esteem, which encourages further involvement (a.k.a. **Adherence** or persistence). However, individuals may define success in very different ways. For example, some people seek to demonstrate competence through improving skills, trying hard and improvement; these are viewed as task-oriented individuals. Those seeking to demonstrate competence through winning and being the best are termed ego-oriented individuals. The role of competence in achievement settings has been studied extensively and can be seen across a number of theories.

Self-Determination Theory proposes that individuals create goals to satisfy three basic psychological needs; competence, relatedness and autonomy. Research has focused on examining how intrinsic motivation is influenced by the interaction of these three constructs. Self-determination can be viewed on a continuum with amotivation (no motivation) as the lowest level of self-determination and intrinsic motivation (taking part because you enjoy it) at the highest level. Perceived competence can also affect the levels of motivation by acting as a mediator. For example, if an exercise class is too easy, perceived competence will not improve and the individuals may opt to withdraw from the activity. Equally, if it is too difficult, the anticipation of demonstrating incompetence may also act as a major disincentive. Therefore, it is important that sport and exercise experiences are challenging yet achievable to ensure the experience of competence.

Another area of current research activity focuses on the notion of self-efficacy. This is primarily concerned with an individual's personal assessment of their ability to perform a task. Individual outcome expectancy (an element of behaviourally specific self-efficacy) influences the motivation to be physically active. It is suggested that there are four sources of information which endow an individual with self-efficacy: namely, performance accomplishments (previous experience), verbal persuasion (self-talk, reinforcement), vicarious experiences (audience observation) and physiological states (e.g. anxiety). Most research concentrates on how self-efficacy can influence behaviour (e.g. choice of activity, success, effort), showing that it is consistently related to engagement in physical activity. For example, individuals who enjoy high levels of self-efficacy are more likely to take part in exercise and receive greater health benefits than those who have low levels of self-efficacy. According to self-efficacy theory, and consistent with recent physical activity research, previous experience would be the strongest influence on an individual's behaviour.

How and why we are motivated is one of the most important factors in determining involvement in sport and exercise. Researchers continue to address the underlying causes, processes and consequences. This introduction outlines some of the theoretical ways in which motivation has been explored and the contexts in which they operate, but these are by no means exhaustive. Practitioners have attempted to outline strategies for engaging and maintaining levels of involvement in sport and exercise from a motivational perspective. While there is some consensus that individual traits, the environment, experiences and significant others play key parts in determining the choice to engage or not, understanding the ways in which these factors interact continues to be the priority of researchers and practitioners.

FURTHER READING

Roberts, G.C. (ed.) (2001) *Advances in Motivation in Sport and Exercise*. Champaign, IL: Human Kinetics.

Weinberg, R.S. and Gould, D. (2003) *Foundations of Sport and Exercise Psychology*, 3rd edn. Champaign, IL: Human Kinetics. Chapter 3, pp. 51–75.

SUZANNE MCGREGOR

Adherence

Sticking to healthy behaviours is important. However, establishing regular exercise, regularly warming up before training or completing psychological skills training can be problematic. This 'problem', which faces all practitioners in physical activity, sport, health and education, is evident across a behavioural spectrum that begins with establishing interest, moves to creating initial involvement and achieves its optimal outcomes by sustaining long-term engagement. It is important to distinguish adherence from compliance. Compliance, which is more ideological than practical, refers to levels of behaviour when the authority of one person (or profession) is imposed on others. Compliance has a strongly medicalised background. However, where choice is the focus of attention, three further interrelated concepts are important; adherence, relapse and drop-out.

Adherence describes the level of engagement with a self-monitored regimen, like taking prescription medication or exercising every day. Adherence has an evil twin – drop-out. Relapse separates these twins and describes the process of not meeting standards of adherence. Occasional lapses are distinguishable from relapse as they are quickly recovered, whereas sustained behavioural absence represents relapse. Drop-out occurs when adherence has ceased. Taking student gym attendance as an example, behaviour may have been initiated in January as a New Year's resolution, whereas drop-out may have occurred by mid-May when other concerns may take over, such as scholarly or work commitments.

Relapse describes the process of withdrawing involvement; it is important because it can bring disappointment and demotivation, despite past successes. An alternative understanding, drawn from smoking cessation is that relapse vouchsafes important lessons to support successful subsequent change. For fitness, the benefits of high-level adherence are also lost during long-term relapse; in physiological terms this may represent wasted investment. Theoretical perspectives provided by the Relapse Prevention Model, which include the essential notion of the 'abstinence violation effect' (which describes the 'Oh, to hell with it' moment), are useful for generating a deeper understanding of lapse and relapse mechanisms.

Drop-out worries coaches, teachers and instructors not least because it is so hard to anticipate or even understand. For example, while aerobics instructors worry that clients drop out from their classes, individuals may simply transfer to other physical activities. Thus, non-attendance, which may simply represent the expression of personal choice, may not automatically indicate drop-out. This example highlights the need for exercise programmers to embrace the notion of sequential, episodic involvement.

One adherence truism is that 50 per cent of newcomers will have given up an exercise regime within six months. Setting aside considerable doubts about the generalisability of this figure, it highlights a central tenet of understanding; adherence is highest for short-term change. This questions the transferability of the '50-per-cent-in-6-months' rule for many interventions. Adopting it as a yardstick may be risky since many programmes may only ever be capable of achieving lower levels, especially within highly pathogenic environments. Further, it may limit intervention outcomes in especially responsive populations; 90 per cent adherence has been achieved for moderate intensity walking five times/week over six weeks.

It is important to understand that the proportion of people who meet adherence targets is closely linked to target demands. For example, a greater proportion of people may walk for at least 30 minutes on one day per week than will meet the same target on five days per week. Since adherence is a process, this underlines the value of follow-up programmes, which address fluctuations in motivational factors such as intention, problem solving and decision making.

Follow-up programmes may also help individuals to coordinate their goals within shifting life circumstances. When residential, work and parenting demands are unstable, they become powerful factors influencing adherence. Paradoxically, these factors rarely feature within exercise prescription, even though adherence is one of its main aims. Lack of time to address and then follow up on complex issues may affect the integrity of intervention delivery and influence the outcomes of different services, including physical activity promotion in primary care.

The perceived need for behaviour within sport and physical activity to change underlines the value of paying close attendance to the factors that promote adherence. While it is important to reflect on the complex interplay of adherence factors, it is also helpful to identify the important individual elements that help to secure adherence. Of the many options for doing this, focus typically falls on three categories: personal, situational and programme factors.

Beyond the evidence furnished by direct experience, theoretical variables also provide helpful insights. For example, the Transtheoretical Model highlights ten processes of change, five levels of change, two decision-making constructs plus a range of self-efficacy domains that all influence behaviour change and adherence. Further, exercise-related constructs are supplied by a range of theories that you will read about (including Self-Determination Theory, Health Belief Model, Theory of Planned Behaviour and Social Cognitive Theory) but that are not addressed here. Collectively, these endorse the value of a wide range of intra- and interpersonal motives, regular monitoring (perhaps including health screening or fitness testing) for feedback, prompts for involvement and access to sensitive and empathetic support. Multiple influential factors underline why the pursuit of powerful predictors has been so problematic.

Theories can assist in exploring exercise behaviour in organised settings, yet frustratingly, they provide little direct evidence of any strategy that obviously improves adherence to accumulated lifestyle physical activity, which centres on making daily tasks more active (such as taking the stairs instead of lifts, walking rather than driving for short journeys). One crucial insight into involvement in lifestyle physical activity is that self-efficacy – situational self-confidence – is a main predictor of change. However, gaps in understanding how to promote lifestyle physical activity have recently generated interest in interdisciplinary approaches to engendering behaviour change. This interest has been driven by the relative failure of existing theories to yield predictive variables for change (e.g. in the Transtheoretical Model only 18 of 40 possible predictors were influential for changing lifestyle physical activity). Adherence to lifestyle physical activity behaviours, such as stair climbing or walking to work, is currently being promoted through environmental redesign plus behavioural prompting. Other approaches involve identifying behavioural clusters (e.g. diet plus media use plus shopping behaviours) that inform how best to support a physically active lifestyle. Still other approaches operate on the basis that the waves of contact with different professionals eventually influence the malleable moments within an individual's life.

FURTHER READING

Marcus, B. and Forsyth, L.-A.H. (2002) *Motivating People to be Physically Active*. Leeds: Human Kinetics Europe.

Plotnikoff, R.C., Hotz, S.B., Birkett, N.J. and Courneya, K.S. (2001) 'Exercise and the transtheoretical model: A longitudinal test of a population sample', *Preventive Medicine*, 33: 441–52.

JIM MCKENNA
ANDY PRINGLE

Physical Activity and Mental Health

Although research into the mental health effects of physical activity now spans four decades, it is within the last 15 years or so that the majority of studies have been conducted and published. Some of the earliest research during the 1970s and 1980s explored the psychological 'feelgood' effects of exercise, which regular exercisers often describe, in an effort to document and account for the way in which some people experience improved mood through various forms of physical activity. Since the late 1980s researchers have been exploring the potential of exercise to reduce diagnosed mental health problems.

A clear trend in this research, which continues to the present day, is a focus on the potential of various forms of physical activity to alleviate the symptoms of mental health problems such as depression and anxiety. Researchers have sought to answer the question 'Is exercise effective in reducing the symptoms of depression/anxiety?' and, even though many studies have been published, the results are far from unequivocal. Together, the findings show that the relationship between exercise and mental health is complex. Although it is probably fair to say that most reviews of this literature are positive regarding the potential of exercise to alleviate the symptoms of depression and anxiety, several reviews also question such positive conclusions on grounds such as methodological adequacy.

It is also increasingly apparent that symptom alleviation is only one part of the picture. In recent years a small, but significant, body of research has explored the ways in which exercise might contribute to mental health in other ways, such as through promoting a positive mental attitude. In this regard, researchers have begun to explore the ways in which regular physical activity might: (i) improve quality of life, self-esteem, or day-to-day mood of people with and without mental health problems; (ii) help prevent the onset or re-occurrence of mental health problems; (iii) contribute to the social well-being of people with and without mental health problems. Again, the majority of work suggests that, under certain circumstances at least, exercise can have a positive effect in these terms.

The potential of exercise to contribute 'positives' (as opposed to alleviating problems) has perhaps been most clearly explored in recent studies, which have focused on the role physical activity might play in recovery from severe, psychotic forms of mental illness such as schizophrenia. Paradoxically, despite their often severe and debilitating symptoms, 'survivors' of serious mental illness often argue that recovery does not depend upon, or even require, the alleviation of symptoms. Numerous first-person accounts of recovery highlight that, while symptom alleviation is important, recovery depends on more holistic factors related to repairing the damage caused by the catastrophic socio-cultural and personal consequences of serious mental illness. These accounts frequently identify the need to rebuild one's sense of self and identity, find new meaning and purpose in life, and regenerate hopes and dreams which have been destroyed through the experiences accompanying mental illness.

Recent research from this perspective suggests that involvement in sport and exercise can, for some people at least, be a significant and valued activity through which these kinds of goals are achieved. For example, sport and exercise help some people to create, and share with others, more positive stories of their lives, thereby resisting the more negative and dominant storylines that frequently accompany serious mental illness. It appears that through narrative psychological processes of this kind, physical activity can come to hold personal meaning for some people which, in turn, brings a sense of purpose to their lives while helping to preserve or rebuild a more hopeful and optimistic sense of self and identity.

A key finding which has emerged through a variety of research approaches is that the effects of physical activity on mental health are individual-specific phenomena. While quantitative researchers working in the positivist paradigm have striven to generate general statements and propositions concerning the exercise–mental health relationship, such 'neat' answers have proven illusive. Other researchers have suggested that such nomothetic studies mask the unique ways in which different people are psychologically affected by physical activity, leading to growing calls for idiographic, interpretive approaches. Here, rather than attempting to predict and control the ways in which groups of people may be mentally affected by exercise, researchers generate rich insights into the diverse ways in which physical activity is experienced at the individual level.

The most recent research that has taken this kind of approach suggests that the psychological effects of physical activity are strongly interrelated with each individual's biographical background, the socio-cultural context in which she or he is immersed, and the meaning that physical activity holds (or doesn't hold) in the person's life. This work suggests that standardised 'prescriptions' of exercise type, frequency, duration, and intensity are likely to prove irrelevant to many people and thus result in limited mental health benefits.

For practice to be best informed and for beneficial physical activity opportunities to be made available to people with mental health difficulties, it is apparent that other approaches such as case studies, evocative stories of personal subjective experience, and qualitative (or 'interpretive') methodologies need to be valued alongside more traditional research approaches. It is only through a combination of these diverse orientations to research that we can hope to unravel complex questions such as: How does physical activity affect mental health? In what ways are its effects related to personal psychological and socio-cultural issues? What are the qualities of 'good' physical activity experiences? How might physical activity be tailored to the needs of different people with unique mental health difficulties? In what ways and under what conditions might physical activity threaten mental health? How might the social, cultural and economic barriers to physical activity among people with mental health problems be overcome?

FURTHER READING

Biddle, S.J.H. and Mutrie, N. (2007) *Psychology of Physical Activity: Determinants, Well-being and Interventions*, 2nd edn. London: Routledge.
Falkner, G. and Taylor, A. (eds) (2006) *Exercise, Health and Mental Health: Emerging Relationships*. London: Routledge.

DAVID CARLESS

Immediate Emotional and Affective Responses to Exercise

If you were to survey members of your family and friends about their reasons for taking part in exercise, a number may respond by saying that exercise makes them 'feel good'. However, for those that don't take part in regular exercise, the reasons offered could include 'exercise makes me feel bad'. Understandably, interest in the relationship between acute exercise and this affect has generated a considerable body of research over the last three decades. This entry will provide a brief overview of the literature, paying close attention to the research processes employed to examine this complex and multifaceted relationship.

In practical settings terminology has often been used too liberally and theorists caution that the distinctions between affective constructs, although not unanimous, are important. In exercise **Psychology** literature, affect, mood, emotion, psychological well-being and feelings are all used interchangeably whereas there is a need to establish their conceptual distinctiveness.

Emotions are specific feeling states generated in reaction to certain events or appraisals. They are typically characterised as being of relatively short duration and high intensity, with a cognitive origin. However, in contrast to emotions, moods are considered as 'diffuse' and lacking a specific target. Moods are not typically associated with the inclination to 'do something about it' as are emotions. Also, moods are generally longer-lasting than emotions. Finally, it is widely recognised that affect is the most basic and broadest construct and any valenced response (positive or negative) implicates affect. Affect has tone or valence, so can serve as a measure of pleasure/displeasure and also intensity (weak to strong). All emotions are affective conditions; however, not all affective conditions are emotions. Further, even though mood and affect can align themselves quite closely, individuals can experience positive or negative affect, even intense affect, without experiencing a change in mood, as long as the experience is not perceived as a portent of things to come. Basic affect appears crucial to **Motivation** and therefore the inclination to move forward or away from anything. Clearly then, researchers examining the exercise–affect relationship should target either basic affect or specific emotions. Put simply, the construct that is most relevant to the topic of the investigation should be targeted.

Although physiological research has unequivocally supported the general advantages of exercise in terms of physical health, the equivalent psychological literature is more complex. The 'feelgood' effect of exercise, particularly aerobic exercise, has been demonstrated through post-exercise decreases in anxiety and depression and enhanced self-esteem and cognitive functioning. However, empirical findings are not always consistent with the message that 'exercise makes you feel good' and the paradox between the 'feel good' effect of exercise and low exercise participation rates will be discussed in light of past and present research methods.

An optimal dose for eliciting positive affective changes is still a subject of debate and the literature is abundant with inconsistent methodologies across every aspect of the research process (conceptualisation, methods and interpretation of data). The construct examined (mood vs affect), the timing of assessment and the self-report tool administered have been variable across studies and methodological approaches have also been heavily debated. A number of the methodological issues will now be addressed.

Numerous self-report tools have been engaged to determine affective change, the two most common being the Profile of Mood States (POMS) and the state form of the State-Trait Anxiety Inventory (STAI). While we have gained much information from the administration of these tools, the POMS is heavily skewed towards the assessment of negative mood states, with vigour as the only positive mood state, and the STAI only measures a state of anxiety. Consequently, authors have concerns that the POMS and the STAI do not sample the full range of the affective experience and this limits our understanding of the exercise–affect relationship.

Researchers have traditionally approached the study of the exercise–affect relationship from a mental health perspective. It is only recently that the focus has expanded to consider the implications of this complex relationship for motivation and **Adherence**. As a consequence, the focus has been on examining whether or not a single bout of exercise can acutely improve how people feel afterwards. Consequently, the negative findings that sometimes ensue from a bout of exercise are often ignored or dismissed as being transient and therefore unimportant. However, one examination of over 45 studies published in the exercise–affect literature to 1993, revealed that, with the possible exception of anxiety, there was no reliable association between acute exercise and improved affective states. Therefore, the focus has to expand beyond the pre-post exercise **Assessment** protocol to allow an examination of the full exercise experience and recent research studies have begun to address this issue. When pre-post assessment protocols are complimented with assessments during exercise, the unitary expectation that exercise only improves how people feel is questioned. The positive pre-post exercise improvement is consistently noted, but affective states have been shown to decline during exercise in a quadratic fashion. Therefore, such negative changes now require systematic examination because these affective changes could help us to develop our understanding of the exercise–affect–adherence relationship.

The optimal intensity of exercise to elicit positive affective change and the associated dose–response relationship is poorly understood. Inconsistent methodologies and equivocal findings are implicated here. Recently, dimensional assessment approaches, based upon the Circumplex Model of affect have begun to feature in research designs because they allow the examination of the entire affective space and target basic affect. The Circumplex Model has attempted to account for differences in affect across a range of exercise intensities in a dual mode model. Specifically, the model posits that low-intensity exercise, below the ventilatory threshold (such as brisk walking), will elicit positive affective states in nearly all individuals. However, the model proposes that these response patterns will not be observed in moderate-intensity exercise (commonly advocated as the optimal dose for positive affective change). Instead, marked inter-individual variability will exist, with some participants reporting positive affect and some reporting negative affect. Further, in intense exercise when participants approach their functional limits (in the dual mode model, the transition from aerobic to anaerobic metabolism is fundamental to affective change), then a homogeneity of response in the direction of negative affect is predicted. On balance, this model may account for some of the variability of responses currently pervading the exercise–affect literature and systematic testing is now required.

In sum, research over the past three decades has firmly established that exercise can make people 'feel better' (e.g. during walking, during more vigorous exercise among certain populations and during recovery from exercise among nearly all participants). However, it is important to acknowledge that exercise can have effects that go beyond this 'feel-good' effect. Further research is warranted that recognises some of the limitations outlined in the current literature.

FURTHER READING

Biddle, S.J.H. and Mutrie, N. (2007) *Psychology of Physical Activity: Determinants, Well-Being and Interventions*. London: Routledge.

Ekkekakis, P. and Petruzzello, S.J. (2000) 'Analysis of the affect measurement conundrum in exercise psychology: I. Fundamental issues', *Psychology of Sport and Exercise*, 1: 71–88.

SUSAN BACKHOUSE

Coping in Sport

There are many well-documented instances where high-profile athletes have appeared to crumble under immense stress. One of the most famous examples was in golf at the 1999 British Open, played at Carnoustie, Scotland. Jean Van de Velde was leading the tournament by two shots, and needed to score six (a 'double-bogey'), or better, on the last hole to claim the title. However, he ended up taking seven shots. This surprising climax followed four days of flawless golf from the Frenchman. This example demonstrates how stress can negatively impact sports performance. Further examples can be found in every sporting setting.

'Coping' describes how people manage life conditions that are evaluated as being stressful. That is, coping involves all behavioural and cognitive attempts employed by an individual to alleviate stress. Coping is not automatic; it requires a conscious effort. For athletes to maintain their level of performance during stressful periods, they must learn to cope using a variety of different strategies. This means that the coping of an archer differs to that of a rugby goalkicker or a downhill skier. Further, existing literature shows the wide range of sporting demands. These range from managing pre-competition anxiety, to restoring high-level performance following poor execution, or managing momentary fatigue or over-arousal, coping with disputed officiating, dealing with a new coach, or with shifting positions within a team or group. It is fashionable to imagine that athletes only need to cope with competition, whereas the reality is that they must cope with training, relationships, careers, injury and setbacks.

Coping strategies describe the ways in which individuals attempt to regain control of stressful situations. They can be categorised into two dimensions; problem-focused and emotion-focused. Problem-focused coping involves obtaining information about what to do and then mobilising actions to change the way the person interacts with the environment (a.k.a. the 'person–environment interaction'). Examples of problem-focused coping strategies include solving problems, planning, increasing effort, managing time, setting goals and seeking information. In contrast, emotion-focused coping is aimed at regulating the emotions linked to a stressful situation. Emotion-focused coping strategies include relaxation, acceptance, seeking social support, wishful thinking and rationalisation.

Many different theories have attempted to explain and provide an understanding of coping. The two dominant theories within the sport **Psychology** literature are the transactional perspective and the trait perspective. These theories contrast strongly.

The trait perspective suggests that people have preferred coping styles which remain stable over time. Regardless of the situation, the trait approach suggests that a person would engage the same coping strategies.

In the transactional perspective, coping is an ongoing process. The individual makes continual efforts to cope. This perspective also states that the coping strategies used by the same individual can vary across situations, and even within the same stressful incident. Most studies within the sport psychology coping literature support the transactional perspective, suggesting that coping is an ongoing and fluctuating process.

Coping effectiveness refers to how well a coping strategy reduces the level of perceived stress. Deploying a coping strategy does not indicate effective coping; practice is often needed to refine the use of a particular coping approach. Coping effectiveness is especially important in sport settings where athletes face numerous stressors; they need effective coping to maintain levels of performance.

Different theories have attempted to explain coping effectiveness. One theory suggests that coping effectiveness is related to the choice of coping strategies deployed and that some strategies will be effective while others will be ineffective. Another theory suggests that the effectiveness of coping depends on the match between the situation and the coping strategy deployed. Problem-focused coping is said to be effective in a controllable situation, whereas emotion-focused coping is thought best in an uncontrollable situation. Finally, the automacity explanation suggests that coping effectiveness relates to the automaticity of the coping strategy.

Sport psychology researchers continue to identify the coping strategies practised by elite athletes. These include a variety of problem- and emotion-focused strategies. Athletes should be encouraged to use a variety of different coping strategies to increase their coping ability. Experiencing uncontrollable stress (e.g. performance), athletes should be encouraged to deploy a problem-focused coping strategy. An emotion-focused strategy is best employed when experiencing an uncontrollable stressor (e.g. opponent's performance).

Coping research has often been criticised for the way it has measured coping. It is widely accepted within sport psychology that coping is a dynamic ongoing process, which changes over time. Studying this process, therefore, requires repeated measures of the same person over time. However, the majority of studies have used uni-directional designs, which ask participants to report past coping experiences, often for the previous 12 months. Other researchers have found that delays between a stressful event and recall of the coping responses often lead to inaccurate recall. There is an established tendency to overestimate coping responses.

In future, researchers should refrain from short-term retrospective research designs and, instead, adopt prospective longitudinal designs. This will allow coping to be examined over time and will generate greater in-depth understanding of how much, how and when change occurs. It is evident that the capacity for coping changes, but important questions remain unanswered, such as why does this happen, and in which people does this occur? Additionally, researchers should conduct coping intervention studies. One reason to study coping in sport is to teach athletes more effective coping. Although knowing the strategies followed by athletes is useful, it is neither clear that athletes can be taught to cope more effectively nor how this will influence athletic performance. Theory-guided interventions represent important avenues for further research.

FURTHER READING

Lazarus, R.S. and Folkman, S. (1984) *Stress, Appraisal and Coping*. New York: Springer.
Nicholls, A.R. and Polman, R.C.J. (2007) 'Coping in sport: A systematic review', *Journal of Sports Sciences*, 25: 11–31.

ADAM NICHOLLS

expertise

Expertise

'Being the best you can be' is popular motivational advice given to those who express a desire to achieve in a particular event or discipline. However, some people attain higher levels of knowledge and skill than others, with some exhibiting high **Motivation** and commitment to this goal. Precursors such as motivation or commitment are important as they may culminate in exceptional human attainment. Witnessing outstanding feats of human endeavour, especially in sport, often leaves us thinking about how these have been achieved and how the necessary qualities have been acquired.

The term 'expertise' relates to outstanding achievement. The study of expertise both describes and examines the growth and learning of specialist knowledge and skill through experience and practice. Expertise can be described as the property of a person ('an expert'), who displays exceptional skill, or the potential to attain what was previously unattainable. In sport, experts are individuals with an ability to execute a desired skill or performance with the greatest consistency and certainty of outcome. This task-specific capability differentiates an expert from intermediates and novices or beginners, who can only perform similar tasks at lower proficiency.

Expertise exists within any domain where a substantial population participates while committing significant time toward an activity for either professional, job or leisure pursuit reasons. Typically, domains involve differing requirements for knowledge and skill. Together, these factors can influence the relative structure and depth of expertise that develops.

Expertise can also be classified by specific measurements (e.g. handicap in golf) or by engagement in representative tasks (e.g. in chess). However, definitions become more problematic when domains rely on subjective or judgemental opinion; in writing being awarded a Pulitzer Prize is an indicator of having attained expert status. Here social recognition derives from existing experts who have also made significant contributions to the writing field. Where the judgement relies upon peer experts, the criteria usually include a long-term commitment to work within the field, with valuable innovations and contributions that modify and progress the domain. In sport, international-level representation is regarded as the general 'yardstick' for being labelled 'expert'. Within large participation sports (e.g. athletics), international selection represents the pinnacle of physical and mental performance, with an ability to consistently outperform the majority of all other home-based competitors. Notwithstanding this definitional debate, one common underlying feature of expert performance is advanced knowledge and skill, placing experts in the minority, often representing as few as 1 per cent of a domain population.

A closer examination of expert knowledge and skill highlights the fact that a distinct set of underlying capabilities become manifest in competition. These are not the popular misconceptions of quick reaction times, exceptional vision and photographic memories often associated with genetically inherited capacities. Instead, many capabilities appear to be learned and acquired across an extensive period through analysis and practice. Synonyms like 'know-how', 'in-depth knowledge' and 'competence' all describe the qualities of exceptional individuals. However, these and other descriptions overlook the more intricate abilities of the expert, such as the deep and expansive knowledge that reflects in-depth understanding. These abilities include superior short-term and long-term memory in their specific domain. Experts notice the features and meaningful patterns that novices miss, while also acquiring and organising content knowledge in meaningful ways for easy recall in a specific situation. Experts are typically faster than novices at performing skills in respective domains. They are also credited as quick problem solvers, showing little error in execution. Experts display varying levels of flexibility in their approach to new situations. They deploy their deep and diverse factual and strategic knowledge to resolve emerging problems.

Experts are also forward planners; they use mental models and abstraction not only to anticipate problems with existing strategies but also to accurately predict the outcomes of unfolding events. Forward planning also couples with extensive knowledge and skills to adjust strategy more successfully than less skilled counterparts. Experts consistently report a greater proliferation of self-regulation skills – a capacity called 'meta-cognition' – which describes the ability to monitor and evaluate one's own current level of understanding and decide when it is not adequate. To address any such inadequacies the expert has a greater ability to implement responses, such as specific training, that enhance knowledge and skill. Collectively, these characteristics highlight the many constituents and complexity of expertise.

Sport scientists have begun to examine and understand how numerous factors can influence the manifestation of high performance levels. These factors were recently divided into primary and secondary influences. Genetics, training and psychological factors may be seen as primary variables, which directly influence the attainment of expertise. Socio-cultural and contextual variables (e.g. environmental climate) are secondary factors, acting indirectly on primary factors.

Training is one factor that has received much attention in sport. The quantity and quality of training is critical to the development of expertise;

the relationship between hours spent in specific forms of training and the level of expertise attained appears to be consistent across sports. Research in music, and subsequently in sport, often meets the established criteria for such 'deliberate practice'. Expertise in sport is proposed to result from engaging in highly effortful training that mimics performance. Further, such training has to correspond with critical stages of cognitive and biological development, and in environments conducive to skill improvement.

In summary, emerging and established experts continually modify the structure and content of training activities so that optimal amounts of effort and concentration are required. This maximises physiological and psychological adaptation. It is suggested that extensive, carefully planned training regimes produce the continual adaptations that help individuals to acquire expert-like characteristics.

FURTHER READING

Moran, A.P. (2004) 'What lies beneath the surface? Investigating expertise in sport', in A.P. Moran (ed.), *Sport and Exercise Psychology: A Critical Introduction*. London: Routledge. pp. 161–92.

STEVE COBLEY

Leaders and Leadership

Leadership involves influencing a group of people towards a goal. How that is done, what processes are involved, what the goal is, and who the people are can all vary greatly. This has made it difficult to study leadership in a reliable and valid way. Defining leadership through 'influence' implies that the leader is central in the group. However, recent approaches to studying leadership have also focused on the people who follow. This suggests that another way of understanding leadership is to say that a leader is someone who others follow.

There are many approaches to studying leaders and leadership. Some approaches identify characteristics that distinguish successful from unsuccessful leaders. Others look at the match between the leader and the environment. Still others have looked at leadership as a process and consider the interaction of leader and the environment over time.

There are two main leader-focused approaches. The 'trait approach' considers that identifying the personality traits of great leaders is a good first step to selecting people with those qualities (using appropriate personality measures). In contrast, the 'skills approach' suggests that (i) leaders are behaviourally distinctive; (ii) that their skills and behaviours can be learned; and (iii) that people can be taught to lead.

In the trait approach to leadership, researchers investigate personality and conduct cognitive tests to identify the common traits of 'great' leaders. Traits are factors that we are either born with or acquire early in life; they are stable over time and are not easy to change or learn. The results of trait-based studies generally show little consistency, although the most consistently identified factors include intelligence, self-confidence, determination, integrity and sociability (or similar variables). The lack of consistency may stem from different samples or different measures or because no one 'leadership personality'exists.

The skills approach also attempts to identify commonalities in leaders. The major difference is that the skills approach focuses on factors that can be learned. Within the sporting domain the coach has most consistently been investigated as the leader and as such a number of instruments have been employed to study coach (leader) behaviours. Behaviours such as delivering clear instructions and giving positive feedback have been associated with effective coaching. Problematically, a clear distinction between coaching and leading has yet to be made. Consequently, no determination about general leadership behaviours in sport has been achieved.

In the more complex 'matching' theory, leadership styles, behaviours and traits should be developed to meet the needs of each situation. For example, an effective leader working with 12-year-old hockey players might need to display different behaviours to an effective leader in a professional rugby league context.

Contingency theory proposes two types of leader: relationship-oriented leaders and task-oriented leaders. Relationship-oriented leaders typically concentrate on building positive interpersonal behaviours within groups, whereas task-oriented leaders may be more focused on the detailed tactics and strategies of both practice and competition.

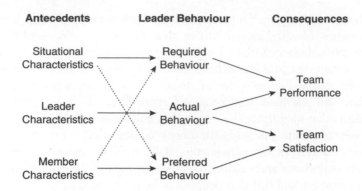

Figure 10 *The multidimensional model of sport leadership*

Situations can be considered on a continuum of more or less favourable, based on the relationships between the leader and followers, the structure surrounding a task and the power of the leader. Theory suggests that in highly favourable and less than favourable situations the best leader will be task-focused. In contrast, a relationship-oriented leader would be the best leader in a moderately favourable situation.

The most popular and well-researched leadership theory in sport is the Multidimensional Model of Sport Leadership (MMSL), shown in Figure 10.

The MMSL model proposes that the leadership style that is required, preferred and that operates reflects the interaction between the situation, the leader and the group members. MMSL also proposes that high congruency between the required behaviour and the leader's actual behaviour will generate high levels of performance. Similarly, high congruence between what athletes prefer in their leader and what they get will engender high team satisfaction. Unfortunately, what is required and what is preferred are not always the same, creating problems for the leader. When all three are equivalent, we might expect high levels of performance and satisfaction.

Research of the MMSL is conducted using the Leadership Scale for Sports (LSS). The LSS is based on the MMSL and measures training and **Instruction** behaviours, democratic behaviour, autocratic behaviour, social support and positive feedback. Research with athletes, about their coaches, has revealed some differences in the leadership preferred by males and females. For example, women may prefer more autocratic

key concepts in
sport & exercise sciences

leadership whereas men favour a more democratic style. Differences have also been found across cultures. Research into the MMSL has many difficulties due mainly to the problems in measuring the various constructs in the model. For example, it is often hard to identify what is required.

At the expense of prioritising the role of the situation, process theories are more focused on following a process by which leadership is established and results follow. These models originate in business and have received little attention in the sporting domain.

This model of leadership aims to bring about change and development in the members of an organisation. The leader stimulates members by engaging with them, understanding their motives and treating them as individuals. Transformational leadership occurs in stages: (i) modelling the way; (ii) inspiring a shared vision; (iii) challenging the process; (iv) enabling others to act; (v) encouraging 'the heart'. Unfortunately, transformational leadership approaches are rarely researched in sport so little can be concluded here. However, anecdotal evidence suggests that some coaches start working in new teams using elements of the transformational approach.

To conclude, there are many different approaches to the study of leadership. Some, such as the trait approach, have been discredited by research that fails to support them with evidence. Others, such as the MMSL, provide a vehicle for our understanding though still need further and better research to demonstrate their validity. Other models exist that have not yet been researched to an extent that allows even a preliminary evaluation of their application in sport.

The future for the research of leadership in sport is bright. Other areas of study, such as the military and business domains, have well-established research into leadership. Looking to these areas will provide the sporting world with new approaches and replicating their methods could produce new evidence for the leadership models best suited to understanding and guiding practice in developing leader structures and development in sport.

FURTHER READING

Anshel, M.H. (2003) *Sport Psychology: From Theory to Practice*. London: Benjamin Cummins.

ADRIAN SCHONFELD

leaders and leadership

Communication

Communication is one term that can be used to describe the two-way exchanges between individuals. Broadly, there are three main purposes to all communication – to educate, persuade or entertain. The skilled communicator understands how to communicate to address these respective aims. Therefore, communication is as important to mountaineers on high-altitude peaks as it is for coaches in playing areas, or friends chatting. The centrality of communication to the daily lives of teachers, coaches and lecturers underlines both the importance of communication and the importance of refining its underpinning skills.

In all forms of communication, whether it is based on 'show', 'tell' or 'ask' approaches, there are three main interacting components; the sender (S), the message (M) and the receiver (R). Each of these agents play an important role in ensuring that effective connections are made and that these lead to the ultimate 'end' for any communication: change. It is crucial to understand that limitations in any of these different sections can corrupt the essence of what is communicated, leading to frustration, misunderstanding and misdirection. Given that communication is only as good as the effect it has on the recipient, we break with convention to reverse the S-M-R pattern to begin by discussing the receiver.

Receivers are the individuals who are expected to respond – in whatever fashion – to any given message. The intellectual, experiential and motivational characteristics of the receiver all play a part in determining the impact of any given message. In any given group there are as many different types as receiver as there are people in the group. The physical condition of receivers may be a prominent concern for coaches. For example, when athletes are overtired they may only be able to receive short messages, being less responsive to longer coaching inputs. Teachers may intentionally tire boisterous youngsters at the start of the lesson to make them more willing recipients of educational input. Once the attention of the receiver is ensured (no small task in some people or settings), the 'channel capacity' of the respective receivers plays a part. Channel capacity – which indicates the volume and depth of information that each receiver can process – may be higher when coaching elite athletes than when dealing with beginners.

The second important interacting factor in communication relates to the message. Here the detail of what is communicated is the focus of attention. Choosing the right delivery form – TV, DVD, example or verbal account – will influence how well a message makes its point with a given audience. Teachers and coaches spend long periods developing clear and simple inputs to ensure that they cannot be confused. In harsh environments, as on a seagoing yacht or on an exposed mountainside, where verbal communication is not possible, the careful practising of communication through hand gestures or signals may be as vital to survival as it is to sporting success. Given that messages may carry many meanings, it is important that sophisticated linguistic practices, like sarcasm or irony, are only used with great care in coaching and educational settings.

In sporting settings, the sender is typically the coach or teacher who has a message that they want to impart to their audience. The sender is the equivalent of the person intending to send a text message to her friend. In this example, the sender decides on the best method to deliver the message and to 'encode' the message in ways that will be understandable to the receiver. This person knows the words that should not be employed – for fear of offending or confusing the recipient – and how to say things to good effect. Extensive attention is often given to the role of the sender, especially in formal settings. Interviews and formal presentations often focus the attention of the sender on how they appear, including what clothes they are wearing and what that 'says' about their professionality and preparedness.

Non-verbal communication (NVC) describes all the unspoken ways we use to communicate. This may convey up to 60 per cent of the meanings taken from any human interaction, so is vastly more important than any other single factor. On the one hand, there is the intentional body language we might adopt to show someone that they are welcome in our company – leaning forward (which narrows the space between individuals – proxemics), smiling, shaking hands. On the other, there is the unspoken, uncontrolled and 'leaked' NVC, suggesting that an individual is not actually welcome; not looking them in the eye, offering a limp handshake, shaking hands but not saying anything or shaking hands but looking away at the same time. Coaches and teachers typically exercise NVC to 'show' technique and practices, with or without an accompanying verbal commentary. Recognising the importance and ubiquity of NVC, poker players spend considerable energy trying to read the NVC of their opponents to gain insights into their emotions. Interpreting these 'tells' yields clues about the cards they may be holding.

Two-way interactive communication is profoundly affected by a number of other factors, including non-verbal communication, environmental noise and feedback processes. Further, in any communication setting, all those involved are continually sending messages that influence the psycho-social environment within which further communication takes place. This interplay helps to highlight the complexity that surrounds, and the sophistication needed, to master human communication.

FURTHER READING

Christina, R.W. and Corcos, D.M. (1988) *Coaches' Guide to Teaching Sport Skills.* Champaign, IL: Human Kinetics.
Collett, P. (2003) *The Book of Tells: How to Read People's Minds from Their Actions.* London: Doubleday.

MIKE GRAY
JIM MCKENNA

PART V

Sociology

INTRODUCTION

It is easier to describe what sociologists do rather than give a simple definition of sociology. Sociologists of sport and exercise are interested in studying sport and exercise as social and cultural activities. They focus on the role and place of sport and exercise in people's lives, how these form both a context and medium for social relationships, and how involvement shapes their identity i.e. who people think they are. Although sociology is concerned with studying behaviour, this is very different from, for example, the experimental approach of **Psychology**. While psychologists are interested in attributes and processes that take place inside individuals – such as perception, attitudes, self-esteem and so on – sociologists focus instead on behaviour in terms of social conditions and cultural contexts that exist and persist outside the individual. They ask important questions about how sport and physical activities are organised and how distinctive groups experience and access sport in different ways. In this sense, sport and exercise are viewed as social constructions – social activities that are created in particular ways. Nevertheless, sport and exercise change over time, and the processes involved with change are of central interest.

Sociologists in sport and exercise are interested in how these activities impact on individuals and their bodies. They argue that bodies are socially constructed, and raise critical questions about how sport and exercise 'make' and shape particular kinds of bodies. For example, powerful ideas about the 'ideal' feminine body lead some women to take part in extreme amounts of exercise in order to try to lose weight and achieve this desired shape.

In this section you will learn about some of the key concepts in the sociology of sport and exercise that help understand these as social practices – **Class**; **Gender**; **'Race' and Ethnicity**; **Disability**; **The Body**; **Identity** and **Globalisation**.

ANNE FLINTOFF

Class

Historians such as Tony Mason, Richard Holt and Tony Collins all use class differences to explain the growth and development of modern sport. In their work, England at the end of the nineteenth century was in the midst of industrialisation and urban growth. In the squalor of the cities, working-class men with newly won free time looked to take part in sport and be entertained by others. Modern sports, codified by the upper class, had been adopted by the middle classes – copying their social peers – then the working classes. For historians and sociologists of sport, its transition from a middle-class social activity to a working-class pastime is a significant moment in sport's history. The idea that sport was a diversion to keep the working class from revolution was a prominent one, as Mason describes in his history of the development of football. Collins (2006) has identified the role of amateurism in rugby as a marker for middle-class values, inextricably linked to the perpetuation of public school Imperial culture and the marginalising of the working class, who did not fit in the world of the 'gentlemen' amateurs. And sociologists continue to identify the way in which sport functions as some kind of shorthand to define class and social status: for example, what does it say about someone in England or Australia if they say they preferred rugby league to rugby union?

Clearly, sport has a defining role in creating and maintaining political ideologies (deep-rooted beliefs) of class, though it can just as easily be explained as a site for (limited) resistance to the norms and values of the ruling classes. From the Frankfurt School, a group of social theorists who developed a critical reading of society, comes a depressing description of sport, which challenges Huizinga's idea that sport is the sating of humanity's playful instinct. While earlier theorists such as Veblen criticised sport for being savage, Theodor Adorno and others in the Frankfurt School drew parallels with religion as described by Marx, the oft cited 'opium of the masses', representing sport as a vehicle for the suppression of the masses by totalitarian states. As Adorno saw it,

> Modern sports... seek to restore to the body some of the functions of which the machine has deprived it. But they do so only in order to train men [sic] all the more inexorably to serve the machine. Hence sports

belong to the realm of unfreedom, no matter where they are organized. (Adorno, 1967: 81)

The class definitions as employed in most statistical and policy research come from an economic reading of employment: the socio-economic groups beloved of pollsters, advertisers and politicians. This may be fine to work with on a superficial level, but a far more complex interpretation of what class means needs to be developed in any substantial (academic) analysis of class and sport.

As an economic definer, class was popularised by Marx and later Marxist social theorists, and the working class was said to be that part of the labour force separated from the means of production in a capitalist society. This Marxist view of class as economic difference was not a new one: throughout the historical record, one can find writers commenting on differences of class and status defined through economic power, and in political discourses (critical debates) that informed the work of Marx there is ample evidence of class being identified in this way. While such a crude definition of Marxist class theory does not do justice to the extent of Marx's ideas and the ideas of those influenced by him, it is a definition from which other arguments can be formed, whether they go on to create readings of power inequalities in the class system – where the economic class structure is the principal thing that defines status – or whether the concept of distance from the means of production and control gives rise to issues about hegemony (dominance and control) and cultural difference.

The relationship between the working class and the dominant class can be seen as a hegemonic struggle. There is a power relationship that tries to impose the ideology of the dominant class on the ruling classes. The transfer of sport and the ethos of Victorian amateurism onto the subjected classes is seen, for example, in the development of Imperial hegemony in Wales through the spread of rugby union, and the popularity of cricket in the Caribbean. Sport played a powerful role in creating and maintaining the Imperial hegemony by distilling the culture of the ruling among the ruled. Hegemony theory, which owes its popularity to the publishing of the works of Gramsci – who elaborated at length on the difference between the dominance of a ruling class and complete cultural hegemony of the ruling culture throughout the ruling and the ruled – is crucial to understanding the role of sport in the construction of class status. Hargreaves and Tomlinson say that the concept of hegemony, when applied to the analysis of structures in sport, emphasises both class and cultural practices. As Gruneau claims, sport does not necessarily have to be a medium for the hegemony of the values of the ruling class. It can be a medium for counter-hegemonic resistance, where the ruled react against hegemony and try to overcome imposed cultural values.

One of the key critiques of Marx's theory of class emerged out of the work of Max Weber. In response to the Marxist idea that class was purely an indication of economic status, Weber highlighted the subtle way in which class and status are actually constructed through a number of means, not just through economic power. For instance, heredity plays a key role in the construction of upper-class status in England, so that people who become rich may not necessarily be accepted as being upper class: David Beckham, despite his wealth, is not a member of the aristocracy, and his wife is called Posh in an ironic sense.

Some people – mainly politicians – argue that class is not relevant any more, and its origins in Marxist dialogues have opened it to criticism in the postmodern, post-Iron Curtain world. Yet the rush to declare the class system dead is not merely a symptom of the New Right (political Conservatives influenced by beliefs in a free market): sociologists seeing a changing world have also questioned the relevance of class. Clearly, all too often the analysis of what is meant by working class (and concomitantly, the middle class) has suffered from attempts to apply crude Marxist economic definitions, valid for the age in which Marx wrote, to changing, post-industrial, globalised, postmodern (where people are not limited by social structure) societies (see entry on **Globalisation**). Although the industrial base that provided the working class with a base in the capitalist society has collapsed, there is still something that can be described as a class system in all countries – only its life patterns and culture have changed with the changing economic circumstances. People still think in terms of 'us' against 'them'. For example, the idea that rugby league is a working-class game is expressed by its players, supporters and officials, suggesting that they believe there is a working class to take part in it, even though standard economic definitions may not give such a clear indication.

Most contemporary sociologists suggest that class is a rhetorical construction that provides the source of the individual and collective identity of the members of that class. The idea of class consciousness, or a negotiation of meaning inside a class or defining a class, gives an indication that the concept of class is not a simple economic definition. Pierre Bourdieu developed the idea that class is a matter of what he called habitus: cultural capital or status, where commodification of life has become the definer, and hence class is both displayed and recognised by commodified signs. Any attempt to define class has to move beyond the given definitions inherited from twentieth-century social theory. Class becomes a matter of language and consciousness, of definitions made by the user in an attempt to analyse and understand their own lives. Hence, in attempting to understand the relationship between themselves, their world and their culture, people become conscious of what they are: in research about sport, this identity is often expressed in class terms, and the definitions people in sport make are as much about community and culture as economy.

FURTHER READING

Adorno, T. (1967) *Prisms*. London: Neville Spearman.
Collins, T. (2006) *Rugby League in Twentieth Century Britain*. London: Routledge.
Scambler, G. (2005) *Sport and Society: History, Power and Culture*. Maidenhead: Open University Press.

KARL SPRACKLEN

Gender

Whether we are women or men has a significant impact on our experiences of sport. Sports participation and leadership patterns across the world, for example, show that girls and women are less involved in sport than boys and men at all levels. The concept of gender challenges the myths that these differences result from girls' and women's differing biological make-up. As we will see later, since the 1970s, there has been a sustained interest in exploring gender and its impact in sport, and as a result, a number of different explanations of the concept has emerged. But described simply, gender can be defined as the behaviours, attributes and roles associated with being either a woman or a man. An important distinction is between sex and gender. Sex refers to the biological differences between the sexes, whereas gender refers to patterns of behaviours and social characteristics associated with being women or men. We learn gendered behaviours and characteristics through everyday social practices and interactions – for example through the different kinds of physical activities introduced to us as girls and boys in school **Physical Education** (see **Physical Education** entry). The concept of gender helps us understand how the undeniable, but small, physiological differences between men and women, contribute to, get taken up by and exaggerated through social practices, and how social values become attached to them. Although gender is produced in specific ways in different historical and cultural contexts, it is generally the activities and behaviours associated with men and masculinity that are more highly valued than those associated with women and femininity. Accounts of gender in sport are, then, accounts of gender inequalities in sport.

The different explanations for how gender 'works' in sport have drawn on and reflected the developments and shifts in mainstream feminist thought. Although taking different approaches and highlighting different aspects, all feminist sociologists seek to question the ways in which sport is linked to ideas of femininity and masculinity, and how the organisation of sport benefits men as a group, more so than women as a group. They also share a common concern, not just to describe and explain gendered inequalities in sport, but to propose how sport needs to change to make it more equitable and less gendered. In addition, some explanations consider the contribution that sport might make to challenging gendered inequalities in other areas of social life.

Early work on gender in sport drew on 'sex role' theory to argue that the differences in sport between men and women result from sex role stereotyping and socialisation practices. From this approach, gendered inequalities reflect outmoded attitudes and a lack of equal opportunities for girls and women to participate and to undertake leadership roles. Although important for recognising that gender is socially constructed, sex role theory has been criticised for its focus on individuals and for the way in which it ignores questions of power and control. Instead, feminist sociologists such as Hargreaves and Hall have argued that gender is best conceptualised as a set of power relations that is both reproduced and resisted through institutions and social practices. This work is important because it recognises that issues of gender are not just about different opportunity and access, but more about how ideologies of femininity and masculinity are constructed as unequal power relations.

There are a number of different strands of feminist thought that draw on explanations of gender as structural power relations. Radical accounts, such as those by Lenskyj or Griffin, identify sexuality as the major site of men's domination of women through the social institutionalisation of heterosexuality. Sport is questioned for its role in the reproduction of heterosexual femininity. Through sport, females are encouraged to develop an acceptable 'femininity' central to which is heterosexual attractiveness and availability. For example, Griffin argues that women's involvement in sport is controlled and restricted through their clothing and their need to present what she calls a 'heterosexy' image. In addition, she shows how lesbians in sport are constructed as deviant, silenced, de-legitimised and stigmatised as abnormal.

These explanations of gender have been critiqued for their over-reliance on explaining men's power over women, at the expense of recognising the impact of other power relations, such as class or race relations (see **Class** and **'Race' and Ethnicity** entries). Socialist feminist theories of gender recognise the interrelationships of gender, class, and increasingly race, within patriarchy, capitalism and neo-colonialism. Gendered inequalities are derived from women's class location and the sexual division of labour, as well as from male power. Through the sexual division of labour capital benefits from women's unpaid domestic labour, childcare, the day-to-day care of workers, and women's position within the paid workforce. In sport, research has shown how women often provide the refreshments at men's sporting events; wash sports clothing for their partner's or men's teams; and transport their children to sports events and support them in their activities, often to the detriment of their own leisure or sporting activities. Socialist feminist explanations have helped highlight women's differing experiences of sport, and the importance of talking about femininities rather than femininity. In addition, they have contributed to the shift in emphasis from solely concentrating on women's experiences to looking more critically at gender through a focus of exploring men's power using the concept of hegemonic masculinity.

Connell's concept of hegemonic masculinity has developed to describe a dominant form of masculinity, constructed, conveyed and internalised through institutions and social practice. Hegemonic masculinity is constructed in relation to subordinated forms of masculinity (for example, gay masculinity) but also in relation to femininity. In Western societies, this dominant form continues to centre on physical strength, dominance, competition and heterosexuality. Writers such as Messner, Sabo, McKay and Whitson have used the concept of hegemonic masculinity to explore how men as a group enjoy privileges in sport through the construction on unequal power relations, but also how men pay the cost for their adherence to narrow definitions of masculinity, and the importance of differences and inequalities between men.

Recognising difference has led to new questions and explanations about gender and sport. However, black feminists have challenged the dominant white feminist theorising and activism since the early days of second-wave feminism, arguing that they have largely been excluded and made invisible. Black feminists argue that the sites of oppression may be different to those of white women. For example, many white women have seen the family as a major site of their oppression by both men and the sexual division of labour, but for some black women, the family is seen as an important site for their resistance and solidarity, where they can have control. In addition, by only focusing on gender power relations, white feminists have neglected to problematise racial power (including their own whiteness) as central to the production of white feminist knowledge (see **'Race' and Ethnicity**). There is still little work that could be defined as offering a black feminist perspective in sport. Much of the work on race focuses on black sportsmen, drawing on the concept of hegemonic masculinity.

Post-structuralist feminists have been keen to challenge the idea of structural gender power relations discussed in the explanations above (that is, top–down and repressive). Instead they should be seen as plural and productive, in a multitude of sites such as **The Body**, discourse, knowledge, subjectivity and sexuality. Although relatively under-developed in sport so far, the focus on the body in post-structural work more generally signals its relevance to understanding gender and sport. These explanations of gender seek to show how sport contributes to the maintenance of binary oppositions, such as man/woman; heterosexual/homosexual; white/other and also for its potential to transgress gender and deconstruct these binaries. For example, the work on body building and boxing shows how women's engagement in sports traditionally defined as male challenges the boundaries of femininity and masculinity through the development of strong, muscular bodies.

The different explanations of gender overviewed here show the richness and depth of feminist work, but also reflect the ongoing resilience of gendered inequalities in sport that still require challenge.

FURTHER READING

Hargreaves, J. (2000) *Heroines of Sport: The Politics of Difference and Identity*. New York: Routledge.
Scraton, S. and Flintoff, A. (2002) *Gender and Sport: A Reader*. London: Routledge.

ANNE FLINTOFF
SARAH SQUIRES

gender

'Race' and Ethnicity

Because it is common for people to talk about race, it has an everyday quality that makes it significant. In the social sciences 'race' often appears like this between inverted commas. Writers do this to demonstrate that they do not accept that in biological terms there is such a thing as race, but they recognise that, because of the way people have thought over the centuries, a concept of race has been socially constructed. These ideas of separate races are derived from nineteenth-century science and live on in contemporary interests in genetics, though the advances in genetics have served to emphasise just how much we all have in common. Ethnicity has been used as a more helpful alternative to 'race' to embrace social diversity like religion, culture, nationality and language. As such, ethnic categories are often chosen by social groups rather than externally imposed upon them.

Choice is an important consideration in leisure and sport. How participation is expressed can be a statement of individual and collective **Identity** (see **Identity**). Indeed, sport may be used deliberately to create a sense of national, civic or cultural identity. Sport and sports have been said to encourage their own cultures that themselves include and exclude others. At its worst, excessive identification with a nation promotes the kind of xenophobia (hatred of foreigners) surrounding many sporting occasions. The theme of the other (otherness and othering) is one that presents fruitful lines of enquiry in sport and leisure research, as we shall demonstrate.

The sensitivity surrounding issues of 'race' and ethnicity means that the very terminology employed is emotive. Terminology changes over time and place. What is 'acceptable' in one arena is not in another. For example, in South Africa the use of 'black'/'white'/'coloured' would be commonplace. In the UK 'coloured' is outdated, with black and white being the main categories serving to denote political racial differences (the dichotomy functioning to identify those who suffer discrimination in a majority white society). However, these terms are objected to by some from Asian backgrounds because the term 'black' is commonly used to denote those of an African-Caribbean heritage. In the United States the collective term is more likely to be 'people of color'. This might then be subdivided into 'black', African American, native

key concepts in
sport & exercise sciences

American, Hispanic. However, the history, demographics and politics of regions differ and therefore so do the relations in each society. In Europe the suggestion that people from Hispanic backgrounds represent a separate racial grouping would be met with bewilderment. If the debates in other countries have been anything like those in the UK over the classification used for the Census, they too have shown the flaws in attempts at racial identification.

Racism is the end result of racial thinking, typically represented in racial discrimination arising from prejudice that may be reflected in feelings of antipathy or superiority. It is possible to recognise a continuum from unintentional to intentional racism that would include ignorance, antipathy and superiority in regard to the 'other'. Racism is most often understood as the product of the thinking and behaviour of individuals, but is now also recognised as operating at institutional and societal levels quite independently of whether or not individuals within them are being consciously racist – e.g. policies implemented regardless of individuals, like those around recruitment.

'Race' in sport research has often focused on black (predominantly male) groups and resulted in a growing awareness of the impact of racism on the sporting experiences of these groups. Valuable though this has been, until recently this research activity has ignored the processes causing these practices. Drawing on critical **Sociology**, and more recently critical race theory, a focus on whiteness as opposed to 'blackness', has emerged out of research interrogating issues of racialised identities and sport. The significance of whiteness in Europe, North America and Australia is that it goes unremarked; it is seen to represent the norm and leaves white racism and privilege unexamined.

Racial thinking or what St Louis, among others, has called 'race logic' in sport is often perpetuated by four weak theoretical propositions:

1 sports are based on theoretical principles of equality;
2 the results of sporting competition are unequal;
3 this inequality of results has a racial bias;
4 therefore given the equality of access and opportunity, the explanation of the unequal results lies in racial physicality.

We all use stereotypes to allow us to operate in a world where we are bombarded with information. Yet in doing so uncritically we inevitably do an injustice to those who are thereby misrepresented. Moreover, we assume, we presume, we prejudge and we attach approval/disapproval, inferiority/superiority to these stereotypes. Some of these approvals/disapprovals are more significant than others because of the balance of power within society. In sport, stereotypes have been used to attribute particular characteristics and aptitudes to players on grounds of their 'race'. For example, Asian cricketers are 'natural spin bowlers and wristy batters', African-Caribbean players are 'fast and strong', white players are 'hard-working and intelligent'. Some are, but examples to the contrary and players with other characteristics refute these myths.

More recent writing and research have demonstrated flaws in these conceptions. However, in several team sports, these stereotypes were found to be associated with 'stacking', the imbalance in the representation of ethnic groups in different positions/roles. Positions requiring decision making and tactical awareness were disproportionately the preserve of white players. Thus American football saw a plethora of white quarterbacks and black wide receivers and football in the UK many white midfield players and black wingers. Although from time to time such patterns seem to be gradually being eroded, the implication for the individual is that their opportunities are constrained by the stereotypes held by coaches and managers regarding these presumed attributes.

The media play a powerful part in depicting people and so can perpetuate particular stereotypes. While black success in many professions has been limited, there are high-profile black sporting superstars (though still in a relatively small number of sports) whom youngsters can choose to emulate. Given the presumed significance of role models, the power of the media in constructing racial identities is particularly important.

Much of the early research in sport and leisure addressed issues in terms of racial stratification in participation in sport and leisure and was concerned to work out how to raise the participation rates of minority ethnic groups. More recently policy makers and academics have utilised the concept of social exclusion to describe how low participation in sport among groups in society is reflective of low participation in other public facilities and services. Examining the processes of social exclusion forces a recognition of diversity in sport and a recognition that 'race' should not be treated in isolation, but researched in conjunction with other social fractures like class and gender (see **Class** and **Gender**).

Sport has been lauded as a vehicle for social cohesion. There are many examples of sport uniting communities and nations, but there are equally instances where divisions have been exacerbated. Difficulties arise when sport is exploited to exert cultural values on subordinate others. This might take the form of a more sophisticated cultural racism that privileges certain affiliations or values over others (e.g. in defence of 'what it means to be British'). For example, in the UK Lord Tebbitt urged all citizens, regardless of origin, to support the sporting teams of their country of residence rather than familial background. This viewpoint had the effect of subjugating or diluting other cultural values and associations while privileging more traditional 'imagined communities'. More generally over the past 30 years or so, UK public bodies have tended to favour a policy of multiculturalism and recognising diversity. If carried into leisure policy, this would mean an equal valuing of the leisure interests (the arts and sport) of black and minority ethnic groups.

Despite protestations of equality within sport, successive studies have revealed varying levels of racism in sport. Hence sport has sometimes been the site of anti-racism campaigns, sometimes at the instigation of the respective national governing bodies and sometimes despite them. There has been some measure of success despite criticism from left and right. They are attacked by conservatives for creating a problem where one did not previously exist or for blaming sport for something that is society's problem; they are criticised by radicals for being too liberal or piecemeal or for focusing on 'hooligans' rather than on more fundamental structural issues.

Carrington, and Williams and Giulianotti have been among those who have sought to demonstrate that sport is a site of struggle for minority ethnic groups, offering opportunities for resistance through helping to promote black consciousness and creating alternatives to the mainstream. However, questions remain as to how extensive that challenge can really be.

FURTHER READING

Carrington, B. and McDonald, I. (2001) *Race, Sport and British Society*. London: Routledge.
Sociology of Sport Journal (2005) *Special Issue on Whiteness*, 22 (3), September.

Jonathan Long
Kevin Hylton

Internationally, research consistently reports that disabled people participate less and undertake a narrower range of sporting activities than non-disabled people. A range of factors has been held responsible for this situation, including the fact that participants suffer from a lack of support, accessible facilities and equipment. Some disabled people also argue that stereotypical and discriminatory assumptions held by non-disabled people deter them from actively engaging in sport. As I discuss later, disability is a fluid concept and has been understood in different ways over time. Importantly, these differing conceptions of disability have wider implications for the ways in which disabled people are perceived, treated and positioned within society, and more specifically located within the practice of sport. As a consequence of these different understandings of disability, the relationship between sport and disability is not a simple one and has been described by Steadward as 'contradictory and complex'. The contradiction is evidenced through the images of elite, non-disabled sports performers found in the popular media that extensively focus on finely tuned athletes boasting immense ability and supreme physical prowess. Contrast these images with dominant understandings of disability, which often locate disabled people as needing care, passive and defective in some way – images that are very distant from those associated with elite sport. The complexity relating to Steadward's observation is that disabled people can and do participate in sport and may exhibit characteristics similar to their non-disabled counterparts that demonstrate ability and physical prowess. By viewing sport through the lens of disability, DePauw argues that this allows us to problematise the socially constructed nature of sport and highlight the ways in which the practice of sport may not currently best serve many people, including those with a disability, to engage in sporting activity.

Two dominant views of disability continue to influence thinking and understandings of disability and what it is to be disabled. From one perspective disability is seen as a naturalistic form, focused on the individual and defined in medical terms. This 'medical' model of disability emerged during the twentieth century and during this time medical specialists sought to 'help' disabled people to cope, or fit in, with 'normal' life. From this perspective, a disabled person is regarded as deficient and the non-disabled norm is considered the more favourable position to occupy. The historical development of sport for disabled people has also been influenced by this medicalised understanding of disability and in this context sport was, and continues to be, used as a vehicle serving therapeutic and rehabilitative ends. Meanwhile, research activity has also centred on medically oriented understandings of disability and investigated physiological, biomechanical and motor developmental dimensions of sport relating to disability. Within this particular body of research disabled people have largely been treated as objects to be experimented and researched on.

In contrast to the medical model of disability, a second alternative view of disability emerged in the 1970s that challenged this deficit and individualised understanding of disability. The 'social model' of disability was developed by disabled activists and academics in response to their dissatisfaction with the way in which disability was conceived through the medical model. Over the past three decades the body of literature emerging from writers supporting a social model perspective has become recognised as a field of study in its own right, known as 'disability studies'. Advocates of the social model, such as Finkelstein and Oliver, believe that people with impairments are disabled by a society that is not organised and structured in ways that take account of differing needs. For example, sports centres with inaccessible buildings, unclear written materials and staff with discriminatory attitudes disable people with impairments. From this social model perspective, these conditions are inequitable and contribute to the discrimination against and oppression of disabled people.

Within wider society and sport the social model seems to have become the orthodox one for understanding disability and is advocated through legislation, policy and programming. The social model then helps us to understand that the barriers and challenges disabled people may experience when they (attempt to) participate in sport may be a product of the way broader society and sport is organised and practised rather than centring on the impairment that the individual experiences. Indeed, even with wide support of the social model of disability, the concern still remains within sport that inequalities continue to preclude disabled people from participating in or gaining positive experiences of sport. According to Barton, sport is merely another sphere of life that is not structured or organised in ways that appropriately consider disabled people. In this context, Barton argues that the very foundations of sport are based on 'ableist' assumptions and little consideration is given to the consequences that this may have on many disabled people who fail to match up to these ideals. Some commentators have argued that the development of disability sport and adapted sport is enabling and signals a move towards more equitable sports opportunities for disabled people. This view has also been challenged and linked to broader literature within **Physical Education** and sport, which argues that these practices require fundamental change (rather than superficial adaptations) in order to enable more people to gain positive sporting experiences.

Recently, a number of commentators have argued that, although the social model addresses broader societal conditions that affect the experiences of disabled people, it does not shed light on disabled people's actual experiences of life and the ways in which disability impacts on their everyday experiences. It has been suggested that this omission fails to account for the complexity and fluidity of people's identities and the position(s) of disability within this (see **Identity**). Therefore, rather than viewing all disabled people as the same, and assuming commonality, it is argued that accounts need to reflect and represent differences between disabled people. Within sport there is a small but growing body of literature that seeks the views and perceptions of disabled people in relation to their broader life experiences and sport. This work though remains overshadowed by the majority of work within sport that focuses on interests underpinned by medical model understandings.

Disability is an evolving and contested notion. It can be understood in different ways and this means that interpretations in relation to sport will also differ and depend upon the view of disability adopted. That said, much still needs to be learnt about the multifaceted nature of disabled people's sporting lives and the interrelationship with **Gender**, ethnicity, **Class** and sexuality.

FURTHER READING

Barnes, C., Oliver, M. and Barton, L. (2002) (eds) *Disability Studies Today*. Cambridge: Polity Press.
DePauw, K.P. and Gavron, S.J. (2005) *Disability Sport*. Leeds: Human Kinetics.

HAYLEY FITZGERALD

key concepts in
sport & exercise sciences

The Body

We are all embodied in that we have a physical bodily form throughout our lives. We know our own body and have expectations of how it will behave in particular circumstances. For many of us, our physical, or *corporeal* body is mostly experienced in stable and predictable ways that we take for granted. It may only be when the body fails to perform in expected ways because we are ill, or injured, or just 'out of sorts' that we question our physical embodiment. People who live with pain, or have limitations to bodily performance due to disease, **Disability**, injury or ageing may be more preoccupied, on a daily basis, with the body's functional capacities. However, even if we take our bodily functioning for granted, we may be dissatisfied with its appearance – we may feel that we would be more attractive, or happier, if, for instance, we were slimmer, or more muscular, or had different facial features or patterns of body hair. We all do *bodywork* to maintain and regulate our bodies. This can range from basic forms of body care that we begin to learn as small children, such as washing, brushing our teeth, and dressing ourselves to more specific activities, such as various cosmetic grooming procedures, weight and fitness training, and dietary practices that we think may help us to achieve 'better', fitter, healthier or more attractive bodies.

Bodywork involves the consumption of commodities, many of which are explicitly marketed to connect them to images of youthfulness, beauty and desired forms of masculinity and femininity, and which represent the means of becoming the self we really consider ourselves to be. This reflects a growing tendency for our sense of self to be reflected in our bodies, and for our bodies to symbolise our connections to what is valued in our culture, and thus our own worth. Bourdieu considers the body to possess *physical capital* that can be a source of income and wealth. Hard manual work, whether by male or female, demands strong, sturdy bodies with the stamina to endure years of physical labour. Sports such as boxing and football have traditionally realised the physical capital of talented working-class men and enabled them to achieve much higher earnings than those available from more routine manual jobs. Today, the physical capital of talented or beautiful bodies may realise very large amounts of wealth for some sportsmen, and less so, sportswomen, and for models, television 'celebrities' and film actors.

Shilling argues that we all engage in what he calls *body projects*, by which he means that the body is never finished – it is always in a state of becoming as we constantly do work on it, and through which we achieve self-identity. Body projects may involve physical interventions such as exercise and diet regimes or, more invasively, cosmetic surgery. These interventions may be directed towards trying to limit and manage the socio-biological processes that act on the body as we live our lives. Playing sports intensively and engaging in various occupational activities changes our musculoskeletal functioning, for example through accelerating osteoarthritis. Pregnancy and childbirth may affect body shape permanently, and ageing involves an array of changes across the life course, such as greying hair, hair loss, eyesight impairment and loss of skin elasticity. Body projects are focused on achieving individual perfection in the form of 'ideal' bodies and increasingly they engage people of all ages and both genders. The signs of ageing are considered to be something to be overcome or concealed, and rapid recovery of the pre-pregnancy body is held to be both achievable and a personal responsibility within the discourses of individual perfection and ideal bodies.

The acceptability and attractiveness of the outer body is increasingly scrutinised and evaluated against cultural norms that privilege some sizes and shapes above others. Bordo talks of the tyranny of slenderness and Garrett of the 'cult of thinness' that set normalised expectations, for women in particular, to achieve slim and toned, but not overly muscular, bodies. These discourses of ideal bodies locate slim, or even thin, as desirable and regulated, and fat as ugly and out of control. Since ideal bodies are concerned with the exterior appearance much more than with the health of body interiors, thin bodies may be produced by unhealthy practices such as over-exercise, cigarette smoking and disordered eating and still be regarded as 'fit' bodies. Even those women who are motivated by athletic aspirations, rather than by achieving a desirably slim body, may impair the inner body as they strive to achieve their goals. The term 'female athlete triad' describes the presence of three related conditions in some women athletes: disordered eating produced in a effort to improve performance; amenorrhoea (loss of periods) resulting from a fall in oestrogen in response to low body weight; and osteoporosis, a loss of bone density caused by low oestrogen and poor nutrition – all indicate an unhealthy inner body.

Both 'sporty' and 'non-sporty' women now monitor and survey their own bodies to identify if, and how, they are failing to meet an idealised norm. Foucault calls such regulated and managed bodies *docile bodies* to describe how surveillance by others, but most effectively by ourselves, disciplines our behaviours in order to achieve specific, desired bodily forms. Women are especially constrained by the exercise of what Foucault terms *technologies of surveillance* and may resist **Physical Education** activities and sports that are seen by them as producing 'unfeminine' behaviours and bodily forms, or that involve the wearing of clothing that reveal what they consider to be less than perfect feminine bodies. Women who actively embrace activities that were once a men-only domain, such as football, weightlifting and body building, may find they are seen as transgressive in two areas against what is considered 'natural'. First, they have moved into the masculine sphere of activity, and second, in so doing, they have achieved a physical muscularity seen as naturally aligned to what many still see as essential maleness. Many women in this situation choose to emphasise their femininity by adopting conspicuous 'girly' elements of appearance, such as wearing make-up as often as possible, keeping hair long – often bleached blonde – and preferring feminine styles of dress.

Men are also increasingly preoccupied with bodily appearances and practices in our consumer culture, and male bodies are on display, open to the gaze of others, to an extent not previously known. Acclaimed male athletes may exploit their physical capital more and increase their incomes further by being the 'face' or the 'body' fronting the advertising of male grooming products. However, male body projects are constrained by what is considered to still be compatible with masculinity. Men increasingly work to achieve a desirable body and consume a range of products in this pursuit but, as Gill et al. show, they are concerned about being seen as vain and overly concerned with their appearance. They are more likely to justify their bodywork in terms of their personal responsibility to look after themselves and their health than admit that they are also caught up in the contemporary discourses of individual perfection.

FURTHER READING

Evans, J. et al. (eds) (2004) *Body Knowledge and Control – Studies in the Sociology of Physical Education and Health*. London: Routledge.

Shilling, C. (2005) *The Body in Culture, Technology and Society*. London: Sage. See Chapter 5, 'Sporting Bodies'.

TERRY O'DONNELL

the body

139

Identity

Identity poses opportunities and challenges in the varied contexts of studying sport, not least because it is conceptualised and applied in various ways. It is often regarded as preceding sporting and leisure choices and preferences; social psychologists depict identity formations as part and parcel of socialisation practices that inform tendencies towards particular activities. Researchers such as Hendry et al. have suggested that adolescence is a key phase of identity formation with leisure pursuits affording opportunities to explore and express different aspects of the self. Individuals seek affirmation of their identity through social interaction and the pursuit of social and cultural competence and leisure and sport offer key contexts for these expressions. Sport and physical activity practices and engagement suggest that participants and actors are likely to become involved with people whom they 'identify with' and with whom particular sporting identities are celebrated. This is evidenced, for example, in expressions of local, regional and national identities that are formed through sporting affiliations. For social scientists the appeal of identity is often associated with its complexity. This may appear problematic to those seeking understanding and explanation, yet identity is a favoured concept because it helps to account for the complex interplay between individuals and who they are *and* the societies and social forms and interactions within which they experience themselves. Identity thus offers conceptual means through which to examine the dynamic link between internal and external factors.

Within **Sociology**, identity and identities have been regarded as emerging from social structures that represent the basis of social formations, that is, external factors. Identity here is commonly regarded as a product of **Class**, race, **Gender** and sexuality and (dis-)abled structural power relations and as a consequence, sport and leisure experience, opportunities and 'choice' result from these configurations (see **'Race' and Ethnicity, Gender, Disability** and **Class**). A 'working-class identity' for example, suggests particular patterns of leisure habits and sporting connections, from male friendship networks, to pub going, to football and rugby club affiliation. Identity has been conceptualised in relation to struggle, resistance and negotiation and identity politics were certainly at the heart of much sociological analysis in the 1970s and 1980s.

The potential of shared and collective identities to resist and confront different axes of oppression, be that class, race or gender, was seen as the crux of oppositional movements to overthrow dominant material relations. Leisure and sports scholars were particularly interested in class and gender as sites of power relations at this time, though identity was generally implicit in these developing narratives rather than explicitly debated as a concept. The work of Ken Roberts, a sociologist of leisure, reflects some engagement with the extent to which leisure experiences are shaped by pre-determined social identities. He poses questions about the extent to which leisure pursuits can be dynamic expressions of identity and suggests that leisure pastimes are only really the outcomes and results of identities that already exist.

Identity has become, more recently within sociology, central to discussions of belonging, community, location and meaning making and basic assumptions about choice and action are questioned. Identity politics discourse of the 1980s has been criticised for failing to engage with the complexities of similarities as well as differences; and notable critiques are presented in the work of Stuart Hall on race and ethnicity and Judith Butler on gender and sexuality. They, along with others, argue that it is more appropriate to regard identity formation as a continual process rather than as a stable or fixed entity. The significance of the interplay between external factors that shape and influence potential and possible identities and the negotiation and response to these that individuals make, is both complex and dynamic. Sociologist Anthony Giddens proposes that identities need to be reconsidered in the changed and changing social, economic and emotional landscapes that make up contemporary societies. That is not to say that identity has lost political importance; on the contrary, expressions of identity in contemporary, globalised contexts remain highly politically charged, particularly in relation to diasporic communities, as considered by Zigmunt Bauman (see **Globalisation**). To name one's identity is still a (democratic) privilege that many communities are not empowered to achieve.

Not surprisingly, shifting approaches towards what might be considered post-structuralist perspectives, have implications for scholars interested in the multidisciplinary areas of sport, leisure, physical activity and active recreation. How we conceptualise and apply 'identity' informs the ways in which we understand the social (and cultural) significance of 'sport'. Deconstructing identity opens up new areas of research, for example, examining the embodied, gendered and racialised identities of athletes (see **The Body**). Such approaches have notably been developed

identity

in feminist analyses and in critical commentaries on race, where a politics of difference has made significant contributions to our understanding. We can consider the identity formation of a particular athlete/performer and the representation of that individual in a broader cultural context; what images are constructed through the media and what influence does that have on collective identities of, for example, nationhood, gender and so on? Feminist accounts of the body, for example, suggest that there may be new possibilities for female bodies, new and dynamic femininities may be emerging and thus new ways to identify with sporting femininities are possible. This has, potentially, profound implications for how women's identities are perceived, represented and therefore embodied, how they take on a material reality (see **Gender**). However, while there may well be evidence of changing identity for some female athletes, we must also contextualise these developments in relation to collective female/feminine identities and assess the ways in which they continue to be shaped by gender (and other) relations of power, albeit in multiple ways. Identity is thus only useful when it explores individual *and* collective social relations.

There have been some claims however, to suggest that we are now in what might be termed a phase of 'post-identity'. If identities are not fixed and are fluid, self-determined and, to a large extent, relative, can we actually talk about identity in any meaningful way and what purpose does that debate serve those interested in leisure, sport and physical activity? Arguably, there are examples of how sport allegiance continues to signify forms of collective identity. We need only consider the Olympics and World Cup tournaments as examples of this. Undeniably, the premise of allegiance has changed dramatically as a result of technological developments and globalisation (see **Globalisation**) yet there are discernible aspects of shared fan identities. Further attention needs to be given to the range of symbols, meanings and signifiers common to how these identities are formed and how they differ. It also requires analyses of who has access to these signifiers and considers therefore, who does not, lest identity become something celebratory and emptied of value and meaning.

Sociologists engaged in cultural analyses of sport have increasingly shown interest in sports consumption and the extent to which, for example, branding of sports goods plays a role in new forms of identity creation. Work on lifestyle and consumption and in particular, conceptualisations of 'lifestyle sports' engages with critical questions about changing youth, cultural and subcultural identities. A range of 'sports' including surfing and skateboarding are construed not simply as activities but as significant sites of meaning and identity for participants; personal investments in becoming and *being* a boarder for example, imply more than just *doing*. Again, this requires attention to different modes of access and the ways in which sporting identities may be exclusive, resonating with earlier concerns that identity is not simply freely chosen.

This short introduction illustrates how identity has been significant in social science approaches to leisure, sport and physical activity. Further work and investigation into identity seems inevitable as many new questions appear to be emerging, as well as the persistent ones that remain. Interest in identity for sports scholars is not necessarily about where identity originates in social life; rather it is examining its complex and competing expressions.

FURTHER READING

Jarvie, G. (2006) *Sport, Culture and Society: An Introduction*. London: Routledge.
Wheaton, B. (ed.) (2004) *Understanding Lifestyle Sports: Consumption, Identity and Difference*. London: Routledge.

BECCY WATSON

Globalisation

Globalisation is an attractive and ubiquitous idea. It is a concept increasingly deployed by intellectuals, politicians and policy makers, by media journalists and ordinary people to describe and explain processes of change. We live in a 'borderless world', or, more pessimistically as Giddens describes it, a 'runaway world' where change is everywhere. There are pessimistic policy debates about population size, the world's health, ecological sustainability and climate change. But commentators optimistically highlight new technologies such as computing, satellite communication and Internet systems that can transform markets and businesses, politics and military security, personal and community relations and not least, culture and tradition.

Robertson has argued that globalisation is a general mode of discourse, a distinctive way of thinking about the unity of humankind on planet earth. Sports and leisure events such as Band Aid and Live 8 concerts, football World Cups and the Olympics are clear expressions of such unity and global interconnectedness. Media around the world, particularly through advertising and sponsorship, have invested heavily in staging and reporting mega-events around the world. Similarly cities, national states and continents have competed for an opportunity to host such prestigious events. Some experts talk of the 'Murdochisation' of sport to emphasise the impact that satellite television has had in commodifying, commercialising and 'spectacularising' sport forms and sporting timetables. One only needs to look at football, cricket and rugby league in the UK and soccer, baseball, basketball and ice hockey in North America for examples of this.

Previous models of understanding how the world worked, in the 1960s and 1970s focused on continental geography and spatial differentiation. The globe was divided into the main compass bearings of North and South, West and East. Polarisation was central to understanding a world in which the 'North' (USA, Europe) dominated world markets and benefited from trade exchanges that produced dependency relationships and so maintained economic under-development in the 'South' (developing countries in Africa, Latin America and South East Asia). In the Cold War period, there were deep political divisions between liberal democracies in the West and the state-socialist republics of the USSR in the East. This competition also found its way into international sport as 'the soviet road to the Olympics' sought to assert its supremacy by topping medal tables in summer and winter Olympic sports.

Marxist writers analysed the world economy in three 'worlds'. The first world of developed nations constituted the industrial core of knowledge, technological innovation, commerce and financial services. The third world represented nations at the periphery of the world economy, usually producing raw materials and foodstuffs in an unequal relationship of trade in which all benefits went back to the first world. The semi-periphery of the second world was made up of state-socialist command economies, driven by state planning and production targets, which struggled to compete in industrial and manufacturing markets. This global division of labour produced nation states that had to compete within a worldwide capitalist system with market disciplines of productivity, profitability, flexibility, capital accumulation and speculation in currency exchange rates. This model has been used to describe the strategies of global firms, transnational corporations that market, produce and distribute sports/leisure goods and services. For instance, Nike shoes have been produced or 'outsourced' very cheaply in many developing economies in South Asia; trainers are worn and endorsed by global celebrities, notably Michael Jordan, but profits from such 'value-added' branded sportswear, framed by slogans such as 'Just do it', remain firmly rooted in the USA.

Globalisation not only encouraged people to think about differential impacts at local, national and international (or more accurately at transnational) levels but also about six separate dimensions of global processes – *ecological, technological, cultural, social, political and economic*.

There has been growing awareness of the *ecological* environment and the global impact of human activities upon a fragile, finite and interdependent biosphere. The issues around population growth, depletion and degradation of natural resources, pollution and the contamination of cities, and not least, global climatic changes and water shortages, have been highlighted by environmentalist or 'green' politics. Environmentalists demand conservation measures, controls on tourism, traffic and environmental pollution, sustainable economic growth and recycling measures. International pollution, floods, tsunamis, hurricanes, floods and famines, increasingly drive home the point that we live in one world. International agencies, nation states, regions and individuals need to adhere to the green slogan of 'act local, think global'. Sports tourism becomes questionable.

Social action groups and political movements have thus tended to transcend the local and to make common cause at a transnational scale. Some of this activity has been facilitated as the past generation has witnessed a revolution in global *technology*. The very phrase the *World Wide Web* signifies a global network that now transcends language communities, regions, nation states and continents. Bill Gates's Microsoft Corporation and Rupert Murdoch's News International are not only transnational companies, but also carry more global and economic power than national politicians, who head individual nation states only temporarily. Spatial distance no longer inhibits communication flows and information exchanges, as new technological hardware such as computers, tied into cable and satellite networks, compress time and space and permit instant access to worldwide information sites, including tourist destinations, sports news and leisure options. In addition, mass communications – digital radio and TV, CDs and DVDs, terrestrial phones, newspapers and magazines, as well as miniaturised personal networks viz. ipods and mobile phones/cameras, facilitate what Anthony Giddens terms the 'disembedding of time and space'. People are no longer tied into local social networks, timetables and cultures, as they were one or two generations ago.

This brings us to the third element of globalisation – that of *cultural* transformation, particularly, the decline of tradition. Exclusive traditional rituals, folk-based routines, established sports and regional ideologies have been exposed to the influence of global communications and global markets. Traditional and religious authority no longer commands the same unquestioning loyalty and respect. Cultural values can no longer be contained and constrained within a single nation state. Boundaries become increasingly porous as they experience growing flows of people, culture, information, goods and services. Appadurai has pointed to disjunctures in global culture because of diverse flows of people, ideas, media as well as finance and technology. Gilroy describes these mixtures as cultural hybridity. One should not think solely of the roots of culture as shared ethnic history, distinctive common language, shared sports and unique heritage of dates and landscapes but also as transatlantic routes leading to the mix of 'black' and 'white' cultures. Migrations of footballers to the UK Premiership, set up with Murdoch's investment for media rights, are often quoted as examples of just such hybridity. Soccer teams such as Arsenal, Chelsea and Bolton Wanderers have been filled with global celebrities rather than 'local' players (however defined, although the popular media have drawn boundaries between 'English' and 'foreign' players).

Closely linked to cultural changes are the *social* transformations taking place that have loosened the constraints of traditional institutions and local communities on individuals. In these 'new times' individuals are forced to choose between varieties of domestic forms. Social networks, particularly within UK households, become more fragmented, flexible and diverse. Marriage and the family are no longer necessarily sequential, as the percentage of single parents increases and there are legal civil partnerships for same-sex couples. Marriage can be deferred into partner relationships and divorce beckons for nearly half of contemporary UK marriages. Household patterns become more complex with longevity, mobility, diversity of lifestyles and sexual identities encouraging some couples to search for stability outside traditional heterosexual relationships. Reshaping the family at global level, there is what Giddens terms 'a democracy of emotions', as gender relations change and women collectively gain more autonomy from traditional family roles, formerly ascribed to them by traditional cultures. The individual, both male and female, is confronted with greater personal choice in a quest for intimacy in relationships, and for consumption in lifestyle, sports, leisure, diet and exercise regimes.

Another important expression of *political* change is the growing importance of transnational institutions and agencies, such as the European Union and the United Nations. Individual states have diluted their national sovereignty with economic, health, social and environmental policies shaped and developed in Brussels and elsewhere. The nation state is seen to be too small for big policy decisions and too big for small decisions. Consequently, the power and boundaries of the nation state are slowly being redrawn, as both global and local institutions set agendas and win new policy functions and undermine old arrangements. Policy and political impacts become decentred as there is no longer a single focus or location of power; no single political institution or network of organisations which can take control of, or exercise, undisputed authority over all dimensions of decision making. Nowhere is this clearer than in the military world order. Nation states become less secure containers of power as US military might seeks some kind of international coalition to fight not another nation state (e.g. the Soviet Union, as in the past), but to pursue a 'war against global terror', to defeat loose and elusive networks of active cells that are trained in one nation state, but deployed to fight elsewhere.

Economic changes are clearly also at work in altering global patterns of investment, production, distribution and consumption. Developing economies emerged in the Far East in the 1980s and many of the centres of industrial production, technological innovation and financial services shifted towards South East Asia and China. While labour remains local and rooted in its historical locations, capital becomes footloose, no longer tied to particular regions or nation states, constantly searching for new markets and places that may prove more profitable. Consequently, many regions in the advanced countries became underdeveloped, with lack of public and private investment, high levels of unemployment and social dislocation, gathering pace in a vicious downward spiral of de-industrialisation and economic decline.

It is important to remember the several processes or dimensions of globalisation. There are distinctive and increasing global flows of finance, capital, technology, ideas, culture, information and not least people. But it is essential not to run away with the idea that globalisation is irresistible and inevitable. Although there is much academic debate about globalisation and its changing impact on everyday life, increased flows in one sphere, say in economic life, may not necessarily mean increasing flows in social, political or cultural life. Glocalisation is a clumsy term to capture the tensions that exist at the interface between the global and the local. Globalisation impacts unevenly on national states, regions and cities. Social scientific research has become increasingly interested in contextualising theory in terms of history, place and people. In sport and leisure, traditional divisions of class, gender, race and age mediate the power relations of global change (see **Class**, **Gender** and **'Race' and Ethnicity**).

FURTHER READING

Horne, J. (2006) *Sport in Consumer Culture*. Basingstoke: Palgrave Macmillan.
Miller, T., Lawrence, G., McKay, J. and Rowe, D. (2001) *Globalization and Sport*. London: Sage.

PETER BRAMHAM

key concepts in
sport & exercise sciences